Living After Loss

A Soulful Guide to Freedom

Melanie Phillips

Published by Be The Light Publishing, May, 2018

ISBN: 9781775336105

Editor: Nina Shoroplova and Danielle Anderson
Typeset: Claudia Richey
Book Cover Design: Claudia Richey
Portrait Photographer: **Ishta Devi**

DISCLAIMER: This book discusses various healing methods and spiritual techniques utilized by the author. It does not recommend any medical or spiritual course of action for your specific needs. For any medical concerns, and prior to following any alternate methods of healing, please first consult your medical and spiritual practitioners of choice.

Readers of this publication agree that neither Melanie Phillips nor her publisher will be held responsible or liable for damages that may be alleged or resulting directly or indirectly from their use of this publication. All external links are provided as a resource only and are not guaranteed to remain active for any length of time. All opinions in this book are those of the author.

To all those who have suffered and will suffer, there is a way through. Don't give up. Your life is so valuable and meaningful.

Thank you to my loving family and to all of the angels who walked with me through my darkest nights.

Acknowledgements

Words cannot express my gratitude for the friends and family who have been by my side during my darkest days. Thank you for witnessing me in my pain and loving me unconditionally. Your love and support tethered me here and inspired me to reclaim my life.

Thank you to my loving family: Shirley and Lou, Richard, Peter and Teresa.

I love you all.

Deepest love for my angels here, who had the strength and willingness to walk the dark path with me, holding a light: Lalitadevi, Ali Denham, Joni Louie, Britt B. Steele, Jenny McLean Noble, Nevah, David Raphael, Swan, Kate Potter, Anuradha, Zoe Read, Andrea Keevil, Nicole Marcia, Gwen Nagano, Zoe Eakle, Mantrajyoti, Al Beddingfield, Sachia Kron, David & Claudia, and, Shannon and Farley.

And to Mick Pearson, for reminding me who I am.

I love you all.

Enormous thanks to my friends who devotedly read the initial draft of this book and offered feedback: Kate Potter, Laura Plumb, Farah Nazarali, Susan Murray, Britt B. Steele, and Marielle Smith. Deep bows to you.

I love you all.

Thank you to all of the healers courageous enough to stand in the truth of the light while shepherding me through the darkness: Dr. Divi, Nevah, Michael D'Alton, David Raphael, Jackie Carter, Kerrilynn Shellhorn, and Krista Hurley.

Thank you to both Nina Shoroplova and Danielle Anderson for your skill in the editing of this book. And to Claudia Richey for your dedication and support.

To those of you who, through my darkest days, held me in your prayers, brought me food, and supported me through your intentions, please know it all mattered. May we all remember that everything we do has an impact, and sometimes your kindness and care may save a life. A smile, a phone call, a non-judgemental listening ear, a handwritten note, a home-cooked meal—acts of love will heal us all.

And my heartfelt gratitude to you, the reader, for joining me on this journey. May infinite love be the home you always remember to return to. I believe in you. I love you.

For a seed to achieve its greatest expression, it must come completely undone. The shell cracks, its insides come out and everything changes. To someone who doesn't understand growth, it would look like complete destruction.

—*Cynthia Occelli*

Contents

Impermanence

I wrote a note, like I always did, and left it on the kitchen counter where he could see it when he got his breakfast. I told him how much I loved him and that I borrowed some coins out of his wallet to plug the parking meter for my appointment downtown.

I couldn't have fathomed the hell that would ensue. I couldn't have predicted that when I walked out of our apartment, I would never see him again.

We spoke on the phone once more, quickly, as he was running late for a doctor's appointment. He said he'd made lunch for me, and that it was waiting on the table at home…which it was.

My beloved never came home that night.

My beloved never came home.

For reasons we will never fully understand, my partner Andrew killed himself that day. The weeks, months, and years that followed were the darkest of my life.

I'm surprised I'm still alive when I reflect on the shock, trauma, loss, anger, disbelief, rage, confusion, bewilderment, and pain that moved through me. It's staggering what we can endure without any notice to prepare.

But life prepares us for life.

Life is our initiation.

My humble gift is to offer you the ruins and debris of this tragedy in my life, because we all suffer. We must each transition through loss at some point, and often it hits us when our back is turned, smacks us down when we think we're on the upswing, and drags us through the trenches to see how raw we can be and still open our heart to love even more.

Having experienced loss in many forms—my parents' divorce as a youngster, my first marriage ending in divorce, the loss of my health to an autoimmune condition, the loss of my inner power to spiritual leaders, and later the unexpected loss of my beloved to suicide—I have had firsthand experiences with tragedy and impermanence.

This book is divided into three sections. The first part reveals the story of my life with my beloved and his shocking suicide. In the second section, I share many lessons I have learned throughout my life. The third segment offers you tools, mindfulness-based exercises, and worksheets to support you through your personal journey of integrating challenging experiences and assist you to move beyond being all-encompassed by even soul-destroying losses.

I share from my experience and what I integrated into my life to overcome and heal from loss and to reprogram my neuropathways; essentially, how I created a different relationship and narrative around *my story of losses*. Take what resonates with you and supports you where you're at on your healing journey and leave what doesn't. Use the book as it serves you best. You have permission to skip sections and engage in a way that is powerful for you.

My intention is that this book will support you, not merely to survive but to actually thrive after any type of loss.

Having navigated the tumultuous terrain of grief and loss, I found that there *is* light. *All-ways.* There's no happily ever after, but there is growth, evolution, and love holding vigil during what appears to be the worst of things.

Throughout this book, I will go into more detail with some practical tools that helped me reprogram my mind from victimhood to empowerment and helped me love life again. I hope these practices and insights will lessen your suffering and guide you through the light and the dark. In this book, I'll be inviting you to look at things from a different perspective.

Please take my words, take my experiences, and let them be a balm for your own hurts, pain, and suffering.

She Said

"Is it all about letting go?"

He said.

"No, sometimes it's about embracing and fiercely moving toward."

She said.

"Oh."

He replied.

PART 1:
My Journey

Chapter 1 - Time Stood Still

I'd seen him on campus—a glance and smile and butterflies flooded my heart as we passed one another in the library.

He was taking a film class in the same building where I was enrolled in some weird multi-disciplinary arts class with a bunch of other eager wanna-be artists.

"Would you ladies like a cookie," he asked in the most charming voice. His striking blue eyes pierced me. "My mom baked them." He passed the plastic Tupperware container around, and my dancer friends and I thanked him. I recall the conversation ended with him picking up my hand and delicately kissing the top of it.

Time stood still, voices and lights blurred, and all that was left was me and Andrew, captivated by one another …

This love unfolded like no other I had ever experienced.

Two young artists, growing in love and life—full of dreams and optimism and so buoyant—we were unstoppable. Our mutual love of nature took us out into the mountains every weekend, hiking long distances to access a beauty that few people knew existed beyond a postcard.

We would trek for hours and push our physical limits. He thought I was hardcore, and I liked that. Andrew, impressed, always said that none of his friends would be able to hack it on the intense hikes we were taking.

In the city, we would explore art and music. Life was so vibrant and thrilling together. We were smitten. After waiting tables in the evening, Andrew would drive over to my apartment and read poetry he'd written for me.

At the same time I graduated from university with a degree in Contemporary Dance, I had a strange growth erupt on my leg, leaving me unable to pursue my dream of dancing for a company. My other passion was travel, so off I went to work and live in New Zealand for nine months, leaving my love behind to complete his university degree.

A series of serendipitous events led me to a yoga retreat center on top of a hill in New Zealand where I met a swami, whatever that is!

I had been living in Queenstown for months with some friends and then on a boat before I decided to go and work on an avocado farm in the north part of the South Island. The day before I left town, I received an email stating that the couple running the farm had to take an unexpected trip home to the States and they wouldn't be able to have me. Instead, I hitchhiked up the west coast of the South Island and ended up on an organic farm owned by a wizard. Amrita was his name, and he had a long gray beard and wore purple flowing pants. He had a twinkle in his eye and was one of the first people I'd met who lived from quite an enlightened perspective.

One day, his friend came to visit and mentioned that they owned a yoga center over the hill. She invited me to stay for a couple of weeks and do a work exchange. I was stoked, as yoga was increasingly becoming a part of what I was most interested in pursuing.

At this yoga center lived a swami with whom I felt an instant connection. I didn't know it then but the universe was lining up this encounter, which turned out to be a part of my journey to a new part of the globe. He invited me to study at an ashram the following fall in India. My soul knew this was exactly where I was meant to be.

I made the phone call home to Andrew from the retreat center office. "Hey babe, the good news is I'm coming home soon! And…I'll be going to India for six months in the fall to live in an ashram."

True to form, Andrew mustered up an enthusiastic and supportive, "That's great!"

Years later, I found out it triggered his issues of being abandoned and left alone, building distrust and resentment.

Chapter 2 - Spiritual Initiation

Ashram life suited me. Landing in India was like a homecoming; I knew that place in my bones. I didn't know what a guru was and I felt allergic to the word God at the time (I thought I was an atheist and a feminist), but I could not deny the heart-opening awakening the ashram evoked in me.

I eagerly woke at four every morning and was the first student in the hall where we had our yoga class. The day was filled with karma yoga (selfless service), yogic studies, and evening chanting.

I had a dream one night about shaving my head. When I woke, I knew I needed to experience myself without the constraints and pressures of being feminine. I freed myself of needing to look pretty for anyone. A tiny Indian man sitting on the ground took out a pair of rusty scissors to cut my long locks off before he shaved my head with a blade, right to the scalp. This transformation took less than five minutes.

I took a spiritual initiation into the Sannyasin tradition, received a spiritual name, and became a karma sannyasin. This meant I was choosing to dedicate my life to the inner path and values of yoga, to live and serve fully and wholeheartedly without being attached to the fruits of my actions, and to be the most enlightened version of myself possible while continuing to live in the world; as opposed to becoming a full-on renunciate or monk.

"Why don't you jump in?" an admired, ancient swami said to me one day as we were hanging up our orange robes on the clothes lines at the ashram. She meant, "Why don't you become a full swami?"

I was torn. My heart was that of a true yogi, but I felt I was supposed to be in the world. I loved my boyfriend, having sex, and dancing—all things unwelcome in the ashram.

Andrew came and met me at the end of my stay before we hiked together for six weeks through the Himalayas. The intense changes I had been through created a discord between us. We no longer knew how to relate to one another. I had a new name, Madhuri, and no hair. My spiritual experiences threatened Andrew, while his desire for partying and hedonistic exploration felt like they didn't fit into the world I'd opened myself to and the path I felt drawn to explore.

We both knew we had grown apart and didn't have any skills or awareness to figure out how to come back together. A year and a half later I moved out of our apartment, leaving behind the greatest love I had ever known.

For years after we broke up, Andrew would appear to me in my dreams, always in the water, which I would not understand until years later.

Chapter 3 - Going for Tea

Little did I know, I would spend the next eight years travelling, living in an ashram, marrying, and eventually divorcing.

About a year after my divorce, I received an email from Andrew. Over the near decade since our break-up we had run into one another a few times in Vancouver, but otherwise we hadn't had much contact.

Nature abhors a vacuum.
Where there is space, soon it will be filled.

Andrew asked me if I wanted to get together for tea. I thought it would be great to see him again—water under the bridge and all that…

My heart was racing, although I wasn't sure why. I walked into the café and there he was, a man. Andrew was a man now…fuller in his body, smoother in his speech and movement, more mature in his energy.

We talked for ages, we laughed, we reminisced.

What had laid dormant for all our years apart reawakened.

The universe brought us back together again; we had a second chance to love from a different place, a less selfish place. Both of us had been through tumultuous marriages, and Andrew was a father to a bright and spirited young boy. Despite having to contain our renewed love due to the backlash from his ex, we were intoxicated with one another, as if it were the first time we met.

One night a few months into our renewed relationship, Andrew gestured for me to lie down on his pull-out sofa. He gently placed headphones on my ears and told me to close my eyes.

He played a spoken word piece that he had written and recorded for me years earlier. His twenty-three-year-old voice—smooth, sexy, and strong—came through the headphones directly into my heart. Andrew stood wearing his favorite purple t-shirt, watching me be catapulted back in time and love: "Late night…no traffic…"

Tears streamed down my face; partly from the joy of being plugged back into the power of his love for me, and mostly for the time and the life we had wasted being apart.

Over the next few years, Andrew would often say, "My biggest regret was letting you go the first time." I would remind him that we both needed to go off and mature and experience different things before we were ready to be fully together for the rest of our lives. He would jokingly tell friends, "Yeah, she needed to loosen up and I needed to tighten up."

One night, sitting out on the deck of our apartment, he brought out a huge manila envelope. He had saved every letter, card, and piece of art I had given him from twelve years earlier. I couldn't believe it. He had appeared to move on so quickly after we broke up. He was masterful at masking his deeper feelings.

He told me, "I never stopped loving you."

I could feel the truth in that. I realized I had never stopped loving him either. Love is love. We were both in awe of this miraculous rebirth and deepening of the love that had been sparked so many years before.

Andrew was the social convener of our relationship, planning concert outings, kayaking trips with his son, hikes and outdoor adventures, and dinners out at hip restaurants.

But mostly we just loved one another's company. He thought I was hilarious—he brought out a sense of humor in me that takes a special someone to reveal. He thought my style of comedic timing and wit was "genius," albeit a little "off color." I took this as the highest compliment, as it was coming from someone who was a brilliant writer, linguist, and jokester himself.

His son lived with us part time and we became a little family unit. Going to his swimming lessons together, hosting birthday parties, playing Lego in the living room, and reading bedtime stories as a trio.

Andrew loved that his son and I had a loving, genuine connection, but it wasn't always easy. There was extreme stress from the dynamic with his ex-wife and that bred instability for all of us. We were affected by her whims and change of plans and the penetrating anger Andrew felt she had for him.

Despite Andrew's six-foot, four-inch, athletic, and very capable exterior, he couldn't keep up the fight with his ex. "She's just wearing me down," he often uttered. We spoke about taking the high road and he was so committed to his son having a great life and positive experiences that he did his best to do so.

Andrew was the eternal optimist, everyone's cheerleader. He would be the first to bounce back after a rejection or a disappointment. He appeared to have the unique ability to take life as it came and always make the best of things. I asked him once how, after almost fifteen years of writing screenplays and not yet having broken into the industry, he was so resilient and didn't give up. He looked me straight in the eye with his crystal blue piercing eyes and almost laughed at me as he said, "Why would I?"

Quitting was never an option for him. He had the determination, commitment, and tenacity of a warrior. He worked tirelessly, writing screenplays and television pilots alongside his day job, doing online course creation for a US university.

During the first incarnation of our relationship Andrew loved to drink and party, but I never saw Andrew drunk on our second-go-around. He would have a few microbrewed beers in the evening; that's about it. But after being diagnosed with the beginnings of an ulcer, he was dedicated to let go of his precarious relationship with alcohol. Coming from a family riddled with alcoholism, he wanted to do things differently in his life. He quit drinking cold turkey and proclaimed his desire to run a marathon for his fortieth birthday.

Over the next couple of months, things began to get hard for Andrew. There was the weight of the relationship with his ex-wife; a huge income tax bill; the company he was working for was disorganized and noncommittal; his friend who was working as his producer got a grant to focus on her own work and didn't have the time to keep trying to get Andrew's work in the right hands; and his family kept urging him to give up his dream of being a writer and to go back to school to become a teacher.

He was getting worn down and beginning to feel his humanness and vulnerability. He asked me for a book to "get to know myself better." He reached out to friends for leads for new work possibilities. Life was weakening him but also softening him. He no longer had alcohol to self-medicate and take the edge off.

I went away and travelled for ten days in the States, connecting with Andrew over the phone while I was gone. He told me he was exercising lots and meditating. I returned home on Wednesday night to a dinner Andrew had prepared and a walk along the beach. He was wearing a Lululemon hoodie he purchased for his third job interview with the iconic athletic wear company on Monday.

He asked me how much he should prepare for his interview for the senior copywriting position. Meanwhile, he had already researched the company, written out ten pages of notes, and done his due diligence; so typical of Andrew's commitment to excellence in all he did.

I told him, "The best thing you can do is have a relaxing and fun weekend and go into the interview feeling great. You just need to be yourself—they're going to love you." This settled him a bit.

The next morning off he drove an hour and a half to his childhood dentist to get his teeth whitened.

Chapter 4 - In the Half Light of Dawn

The clouds set in and, typical of Vancouver in March, the weather became dismal and dark, the sky pushing down upon us. Still, we bundled up and walked in the dreary rain.

Andrew asked me why I thought we had broken up the first time. He told me I was his hero, which I laughed off. He was serious and stopped to make sure I knew it. He expressed how he felt his ex was poisoning his son against him. I reminded him to take the high road and to realize that his son would grow up to know the truth—that his father was a good man who loved him immeasurably.

Returning home from our walk, Andrew asked if he could take me for dinner. I declined, saying it wasn't necessary, given as I knew he was stressed about money.

"Let's wait until after you get your new job," I said. He insisted.

We dressed up and headed downtown to a trendy farm-to-table restaurant where we ate marrow and house-made gnocchi and drank tea. I remember this meal like it was yesterday. Andrew was quieter than usual, but sweet. He paid the bill and we made our way home.

I'm a bit of an early-to-bed girl, so around 10 p.m. I mentioned I was going to turn in and asked Andrew what he was going to do. He said he wouldn't be far behind me.

Sometimes we would sleep in separate beds because I had become a light sleeper. Although I had been a fantastic sleeper my entire life and had shared space with others in ashrams, youth hostels, and tents without issues, when Andrew and I moved in together the second go-around, I often found myself restless and unable to sleep.

We talked about my recent insomnia, thinking perhaps it was the Vastu Shastra (a Vedic Indian art connected with architecture and design) of our apartment, old energies hanging out in the place, or the direction my head was facing while I was sleeping. After exploring all sorts of practical and esoteric solutions, nothing helped, and so it wasn't unusual for Andrew to sleep in his son's room.

On this particular night, after almost two years of not sleeping, I slept like a log. Normally I would be sensitive to every sound and movement in the apartment, but on this particular night I didn't hear a thing.

I woke up before the break of day, feeling unusually refreshed, and made my way to the living room. The paintings on the wall were askew. Weird, I thought.

In the half light of the dawn, I turned the corner into the living room and saw Andrew, his tall body sprawled out on the pull-out couch. *Why had he slept on the couch*, I thought to myself.

"I fell off the wagon," he answered in a half whisper, as if he'd heard my thoughts from across the room.

Confused, I walked over to him and saw his pupils dilated and eyes wild. He told me he had not only been drinking, but that he also took some over-the-counter sleeping pills. "I just wanted to sleep," he lamented. This behavior was very unusual for him.

I was baffled by the situation. He'd gone out to buy booze after I went to bed and I hadn't heard a thing; no doors opening or closing, no stirring, nothing.

I was shaken and didn't know what to make of this. I got him some water and made him drink as much as he could take. I called my energy healing teacher early on that Sunday morning; he said he would work on Andrew's energy from a distance. Shortly thereafter, Andrew vomited and seemed to be more himself after purging the drugs and alcohol.

"You need to get some help", I insisted. "Who do you want to talk to?"

"Dr. Divi."

"It's Sunday; she's not at work today. You've got a doctor's appointment with her tomorrow before your job interview, but you need to see someone today."

Andrew finally agreed to see a counselor with whom we'd had a couple of sessions together previously.

The counselor was kind enough to see us on a Sunday. The three of us sat together. My body trembled. I took deep breaths to try and compose myself. Andrew appeared calm and relayed the previous night's story to the counselor.

"I wanted to die."

"You wanted to die or be out of pain?" asked the counselor.

"I wanted to die," he said.

The dark night of the soul had arrived. This was his cry for help, and we were getting help. By the end of the session, we had agreed that Andrew would reach out to either the counselor or me if he was struggling. He agreed to begin to work regularly with the counselor.

I paid for the session and told Andrew not to worry about the money. "Don't worry about the money," I repeated in a whisper, assuring him we'd get through this together.

I was in shock. Part of me was grief stricken by the very thought of Andrew not being in my life…shocked by the thought that he didn't want to be here. I knew how much he loved me and his son, so what the hell was happening? My mind began to whirl around our life together. We had been having serious conversation about having a child—serious enough that I was taking prenatal vitamins and we regularly talked about our first child.

We came home from the appointment with the counselor and I made fresh juice and a healthy, delicious meal for us, hoping this would help reset his body and do me some good too. Andrew slept and I collapsed on the bed and sobbed.

By that evening he seemed to have bounced back. We had a check in with the counselor and each of us spoke to him separately on the phone as well. The counselor said to me, "If I thought he was suicidal, I would have done a full-on intervention." Right. Good. I didn't think Andrew was suicidal either. He had never spoken about such a thing and was always so enlivened and tenacious.

I breathed a sigh of relief, happy knowing that we could wake up tomorrow to a new day. Andrew would get to see the doctor and head off to a promising job interview that I knew he would nail with his charisma, brilliance, and skill.

Exhausted from the emotional turmoil of the previous day, I was happy to have previously booked an Ayurvedic oil massage for Monday morning.

Andrew had slept in his son's room and was awake when I got up. He was sitting up in bed, typing away on his computer, finishing up creating his online university work.

I slipped into bed beside him. He was physically strong and seemed so serene and steady. My head rested on his heart. Tears streamed down my face. I was still completely discombobulated, jolted by yesterday's experience. All I remember saying to him was, "I'm here for everyone, and no one is here for me." I felt like I was always giving and caretaking in my relationships. Andrew soothed me and held me tight, saying "I'm here for you. I love you. You're amazing." I believed him.

Exhausted from the emotional turmoil of the previous day, I was happy to have previously booked an Ayurvedic oil massage for Monday morning.

Andrew had slept in his son's room and was awake when I got up. He was sitting up in bed, typing away on his computer, finishing up creating his online university work.

I slipped into bed beside him. He was physically strong and seemed so serene and steady. My head rested on his heart. Tears streamed down my face. I was still completely discombobulated, jolted by yesterday's experience.

All I remember saying to him was, "I'm here for everyone, and no one is here for me." I felt like I was always giving and caretaking in my relationships. Andrew soothed me and held me tight, saying "I'm here for you. I love you. You're amazing." I believed him.

I knew that after all the years of being apart and finally getting another opportunity to love one another, create a family, and a life together, that he was steady, despite hitting his rock bottom. I knew things would turn around today—today would be a fresh start.

We snuggled and then I had to go for my massage appointment. I kissed him and got up to leave, closing the bedroom door slowly as our eyes connected through the crack between the door and the doorframe. Then I closed it completely shut.

Chapter 5 - Undercooked Yams

My massage ran late and I had our shared car. Andrew called me to see if I would be back in time for him to drive to his doctor's appointment. Originally he was going to bike there, so I asked if we could resort to that plan as I was still at the Ayurvedic spa; I didn't want him to be late for *his* appointment.

Our quick conversation was logistical and brief. I planned on seeing him back at the house before he headed out to his job interview later that afternoon.

I got home to a prepared lunch waiting for me on the table. It was his favorite go-to dish of rice, yams, and broccoli in coconut milk. The yams were undercooked. *He must have been in a hurry to get to his doctor's appointment*, I thought to myself.

As the early afternoon approached, I began to feel anxiety build in my body. Even if there was a long wait at the doctor's office, surely he would have been back by now. Andrew had laid his interview clothes out on the bed so I knew he would need to be back by 2:30 p.m. to change.

I didn't want to be the paranoid partner, but I was still shaken up from the previous day's strange events. I called the doctor's office and spoke to the doctor's husband, who was the receptionist.

"Can you tell me if Andrew is still there?"

Pause. Silence.

The receptionist's voice seemed to slow way down and reverberate through my body. "He never showed up for his appointment..."

Panic and fear cast over me. I began reeling, consumed by what had happened the day before and how Andrew had said he had wanted to kill himself.

The receptionist told me that legally he had to contact the police department to file a missing person's report.

A missing person's report? I was sure Andrew had been in a bike accident on his way to the doctor's office. He was the kind of person who would call to let you know if he was going to be five minutes late. I called around to all the local hospitals to find out which one he had been admitted into.

No Andrew. I knew something was very wrong but I was also trying to stay open to all possibilities. Perhaps he had needed to clear his head before his job interview and decided to forgo the appointment.

His 3 p.m. job interview time came and went, and Andrew hadn't returned to change his clothes.

The buzzer went, and two policewomen were suddenly in our apartment. Big black boots on our living room carpet. There was no polite, "Should we remove our boots?" This was official; this was the authority stepping in. This was real.

I filed the missing person's report, my body shaking, bewildered. Where the hell did he go?

My friend came and we drove to a beach he loved. I was sure we would find him there, maybe in a state of disarray, but we would bring him home and I would reassure him that missing his job interview wasn't the end of the world.

The sun began to set and he was nowhere to be seen on the beach. Surely he'll be home once it's dark.

I lay awake all night wondering, worrying, struck with fear and confusion.

An early morning phone call from the police (the police, for fuck's sake!) informed me that they had found the car-share car that Andrew had apparently rented and driven to a forested area far out of Vancouver, an area he knew well.

Search and rescue was on it, but that wasn't good enough. I wasn't going to sit at home waiting for search and rescue to find him. He must have gone out into nature and fallen, broken his leg, and been stranded somewhere all night.

I prepared a flask of his favorite tea for when he was rescued and headed toward the location with a friend of his. On the car ride there, I spoke to a woman I know who is a psychic.

"Water," she said. "I see water and struggle and hitting his head."

Sickened, I took this information and imagined he had fallen and was unconscious somewhere. We will find him. Keep the faith. Keep the faith. Keep the faith.

All I wanted was for this nightmare to be over and to have him back in my arms at home.

The police had cordoned off a section of the park and said we couldn't look in that area as there were search and rescue dogs up by the cliffs. We searched for hours in the pouring rain. I prayed for guidance. At every turn, I imagined seeing Andrew, injured but so happy to see us all. He would make a joke and we would all laugh. We would reminisce for years about "his crazy night out alone in the wilderness."

Night set upon us and the police came to tell us we needed to go home. One officer said, "Well, let's have a debrief. I'll let you know what we found and what we didn't find."

What the hell? I had this sense that he knew a lot more than he was letting on.

"Well…we found Andrew's wallet, keys, and a bottle of Jagermeister on the cliff."

My body fell to the ground.

I had a deep knowing that he was gone…gone…gone.

"But you know…" the officer said, "People can walk out of the forest weeks later."

A sick sense of despair flooded me.

The world turned dark as I felt my entire life collapse.

Chapter 6 - The Rain

We drove back to the house of a friend of the family. There, Andrew's parents were waiting. I sat on the couch and had to tell them that he was dead.

He was gone. There was no body. No proof. No way to know for sure.

My living hell ensued, as weeks of daily calls with the police and search and rescue continued until eventually they called off the search. They were committed to having a specialized diving team search the water where they believed his body could be; unfortunately, it was spring and the water was high and terribly dangerous, and there were only two certified people in the province equipped to make this dive. They had to wait.

The rain was relentless...the waters rose and all we could do was wait. A memorial was planned, despite the lingering uncertainty of his death. I clung to a thread of hope for a miracle to happen, for this nightmare to turn around and bring my beloved home.

Within the first week of Andrew being missing, his mother requested her grandson's toys. When I asked about seeing him, she told me that it would be best if he stayed close to his mother at this time. I began to pack up Andrew's son's room: paintings from the wall, class photos, Lego, and stuffed animals. I gave her everything.

My life was being deconstructed one moment at a time. I would never get to see my stepson again.

What went from a good relationship with his family turned into me becoming the scapegoat for their anger, blame, hatred, and violence. The dysfunction in the family surfaced and erupted. The only part of Andrew they had left was his son. They saw me as the reason Andrew had opted out, and chose to erase his life with me from their minds, instead turning back to his ex-wife and their grandson as the perfect scenario to somehow ease their displaced pain. I watched as the disdain they had expressed for his ex-wife was replaced by praise and adoration.

One afternoon, Andrew's family was in our apartment and we were planning the memorial together. His mother grabbed me and took me aside, out of earshot of the others. She began riffing on how great Andrew's marriage was with his ex-wife. She wanted me to give her any holiday photos of Andrew and his ex-wife, so she could pass them on.

The family began to turn their backs on every detail of Andrew's life that didn't serve them. I was central to his life and therefore, the first to be denied.

Chapter 7 - What Happened in a Moment

My doctor, who is also a medical intuitive and was an angel for me during this time, gifted me a session with a psychic she knows. I got on a call with this woman, whose forte is working with spirits of those who have passed over. She didn't know anything about me or the situation; only that I'd lost my partner.

She became a conduit for Andrew. He spoke through her, explaining why he did what he did and how he had felt. It was literally like he short-circuited and made a very quick, rash decision to end his life. He couldn't keep up the façade anymore. He was so sorry to have hurt me and his loved ones through this.

And then, the psychic said, "His mother wants you dead."

I hadn't mentioned any of the initial struggles with his family to the psychic. I thought she was being a bit dramatic, but in the following days and weeks, the energy that was being directed toward me was intense and violent. I realized what she meant; she was spot on.

Police officers came in the night, requesting dental records. Finally, more than three weeks after Andrew went missing, they found his body in the river, pinned down under a rock by the water current.

My body shook for weeks. People brought food that I couldn't eat. Being alive was a certain flavor of hell. Nightmares, day-mares, the shock, and disbelief, he's gone, *he's really gone and never coming back. Never.*

My dad flew out from Ontario to be with me, tethering me to this world, holding me with compassionate understanding as he witnessed my grief and agony and bewilderment. He watched me crumble and forget how in love with life I was.

He watched my dreams shatter in the most final way possible. He watched the life force get sucked out of my vessel. He watched me die while I was still alive.

Andrew spoke to me; our relationship didn't end the day he died. His presence was infuriatingly strong at times. I found solace in his loving energy. But there was a vacuum that could not be filled, reminding me more and more how far away he was and would always be from my life moving forward.

I still have to be here, you bastard. I know you're fine, but we all have to live with this pain. You took the easy way out.

He had become fully wise and loving in his communication with me; this too was painful. It was like we were on either side of a dense pane of glass, so close but never able to feel one another again. Hanging out with his soul wasn't cutting it for me. I felt more alone than soothed.

What happened in a moment could never be reversed.

Chapter 8 - A Thousand Lifetimes

I had to correspond with the coroner. I retold the story to her and she was kind and professional. I wanted an autopsy. I wanted answers. The only thing that made sense was that Andrew was the most determined person I'd ever met, and if he got something in his head, he would make sure it happened.

His family said no, no autopsy.

What if he had some kind of brain tumor that affected his judgment or changed his personality? I wanted his son to know the truth, and I wanted a fair chance to find out everything we could.

Every decision and moment was exhausting and filled with pain.

Friends of Andrew's and mine were curious and wanted to know what happened. It was draining to recount what I knew about the events over and over again to every person who wanted to know. Meanwhile, his family became more difficult to deal with and his mother was demanding, wanting to control everything.

On Andrew's birthday, I realized that his rent check had bounced. I reached out to his brother to find out what was happening only to discover that his family had closed his bank account without letting me know, leaving me to deal with all of the expenses that we jointly shared. Not only was I unable to work, but I also had no insurance to cover not working at times like this and I was left with thousands of dollars' worth of Andrew's expenses.

His mother sent hate mail to his friends, blaming me for Andrew's death. She demanded our television and all his belongings that had any value.

Andrew's family and I all decided that Andrew would want to be cremated. I requested some of his ashes and hoped that his family would bring some for me the day they came to pick up his belongings.

I had asked five friends to come and help take some of Andrew's things to the foyer of our apartment for his parents and brother to pick up. I didn't want to be present for this as my nervous system was shot and his family was volatile and directing their anger toward me.

My friends—a collection of yoga teachers and modern dancers—ended up being the receptacle of verbal abuse that day. His brother was yelling in the street and his mother got right up into my friend's face, saying, "What the fuck are you looking at?"

I was never given any of his ashes; his family made sure they kept every piece of Andrew they could keep away from me.

Tragedy provokes either the most hideous or the most beautiful response from humanity. What at first I thought would bring all of us closer together, that would unite us in solidarity for a man we all loved and lost, ended up being a wretched and ugly mess. There was no unified honoring of Andrew or his life. I would have to do that in my own way. As each exhausting day passed, I felt as though I was living a thousand lifetimes

How is this my life?

How is this my fucking life?

What have I done to deserve this?

Will I ever not be broken again?

Will this pain ever stop?

Will. This. Pain. Ever. Stop…?

The Dawn

The early dawn

Broke me open

Wailing, animal-like

Cold tiles pressing into my face

(That was already distorted)

Reminding me there was no solace, not

here Not anywhere.

Get me out of this body!

I thought I could scream my way out.

I want to die.

How could he leave me here?

Come back, come back, come back!

In an instant it was all gone

Flesh and dream.

In an instant everything changed

Who am I now?

(And what's the fucking point?)

PART 2:
My Lessons

Chapter 9 - Nobody Knows

I wanted someone to help who knew what was going on and who really got me. It was devastating to find out that that person didn't exist.

Where to go when you're left alone with other mortals, fumbling through the darkness? You go to the Creator. You go to the one who you think did this to you—betrayed you so incredibly by ruining your life. You offer up your life to the Divine because there is nothing else you can do.

Nobody actually has any concrete answers.

The wisest people I've met never claimed to know anything. My father sat with me in our apartment for three weeks after Andrew went missing, listening to my neurosis and hearing the pained confusion over and over again—his profound ability to be present and listen without fixing anything was staggering. This was the greatest gift.

He never once said, "Everything happens for a reason." This is one of the most destructive things anyone can spurt out of their mouth at a time of grief. Even if it is true, it must be left to the one grieving to come to know this for themself and this may take years to feel or accept. The truth is we don't know why tragedy strikes.

The empowerment is in what we do with our suffering. All of the so-called enlightened teachers, theories, or philosophies only point the way—they are not the way.

You must find your own.

Loss altered the very fabric of my reality. My entire identity was no longer what I believed it to be and nothing felt solid. My world changed and couldn't be unchanged. My heart was tender and torn open. It couldn't be undone.

If you too find yourself here, in fleeting moments or for long periods of time, be gentle with your sweet self. Your soul is infinite, eternal, and ever so powerful, but the human experience of loss can feel excruciating. There is a way through. There is a way through. In this section I will share with you lessons I've learned through so many of my losses. In Part Three I offer you tools and mindfulness-based techniques for navigating the darkness and reclaiming your life. Remember, take what feels nourishing for you and leave the rest.

Chapter 10 - Layers of Loss

Loss can come in all kinds of ways and various forms. Reflecting back on my life I realize that there have been many losses. As I was experiencing these losses in my life I didn't appreciate them as that, but after Andrew died I felt the accumulation of them all. They were amplified...

The first loss I can recollect and the one that reverberates through all of the losses in my life is the *loss of a dream*.

~

We all agreed that we would order pizza and that Dad would stay for dinner, even though our parents had just told my brother and me that our family would never be a family again. The pizza tasted like pain with a cardboard crust. I stared down at the table, nibbling on food that was usually reserved for celebrations and parties.

Was this supposed to make us feel better?

What was even more shocking than our parents getting a divorce was that I had already heard the news on the playground. In a small town, news travels fast; people talk, and kids don't have a filter.

I was humiliated hearing the news at school and not being at all sure how to respond. It was the eighties and divorce wasn't as trendy as it is now.

Our family was broken.

After dinner I went for a walk with my friend. My little ten-year-old feet stood in an empty grass lot at the edge of town. Staring up at the night sky, smattered with stars, I felt the magnitude of the universe above and around me.

I was devastated yet hopeful in the way only a child can recover after loss.

What was worse than the loss of my family was the loss of my dream.

I was standing in the lot that my parents had purchased. We'd spent months walking through model homes in preparation for building our new house. I'd been so inspired by these gorgeous model homes, I envisioned every last detail of the room I would decorate…the checkered floor tiles and red toilet and bathtub in the bathroom my brother and I would share (It seemed like a good idea at the time. Did I mention it was the eighties?). I would have a bay window in my bedroom with pastel-colored pillows and a canopy bed with curtains draping down around me. I had planned the lap pool along the side of the house where I would wake early and swim my little heart out. I was dreaming and it felt fantastic, everything was lining up. We would finally have a dream home and life would be perfect.

Suddenly, everything was shattered. There would be no lap pool and no bay window. My dad was moving out, our family was fractured, and no one would build the dream home.

Around the same time that my parents got divorced, I became fiercely independent. I marched down the main street of town and signed myself up for a social insurance number. To this day I have the card with my barely developed ten-year-old signature on my official government document. This was my ticket to financial and personal freedom, as I didn't want to burden my parents during this difficult time.

I would pick stones in farmers' fields after school to make some cash or go strawberry picking to save up for the Converse knock-off sneakers I was pining for.

The loss of innocence can be so tragic.

What transpired after my parents' divorce may have been more traumatic than the actual breakup. My mom began dating a man who was abusive. Holes were punched in my bedroom door, bruises were left on my mom's arms, and all this climaxed in the psycho-boyfriend hiding out in the garage and trying to strangle my mom when she went to her car to go to work in the morning.

After that fiasco we got the police involved and tracked every harassing phone call or incident, and a restraining order was set in place.

Where did my childhood go?

Thanks to great friends, a wild and entertaining high school experience, and a genuine inclination for learning and wanting to contribute in the world, I coped. I explored sports and became riveted by modern dance, which carried me to complete my degree in contemporary dance from Simon Fraser University in Vancouver.

The rigor of the daily training schedule and waking up to dance to live music every day of my life was exhilarating. I was in my element. I loved to create and choreograph, and I excelled at it.

In the dance world there isn't a lot of focus on taking care of your body, resting, and making your career sustainable. I pushed; I overachieved—fuelled partly by the sheer love of it and partly from what I would see years later was the shadow of *not feeling good enough unless I was doing.*

In my final year at university, I was already performing professionally in the community. I was planning to move to London, England and dance for a company there, or so I thought. Suddenly, I was riddled with acute tendinitis that left me limping across campus, unable to walk without pain.

The first of a slew of obscure health issues in my life began in this fourth and final year at university. I graduated on crutches with a strange growth that had erupted on my ankle, leaving me incapacitated.

Another dream shattered.

All I wanted to do was dance. I didn't know who I was if I wasn't dancing—the only other thing that inspired me as much was travel.

Experiences of loss live deep inside of us. They influence who we are and the decisions we make, often unconsciously. Honouring our losses, no matter how miniscule we may deem them to be, helps us to regain our power and life. I found that giving voice to my losses—writing them down, speaking them to people I trusted—allowed me to move and integrate the experiences, to move beyond being a victim. Also, working with the mindfulness-based practices and tools that I will share with you in Part Three was paramount to my healing.

Chapter 11 - Depleted

Not being able to dance catapulted me on an adventure of travel to foreign lands, spanning many years. On one occasion, I traveled solo through Asia for nine months, seeing great sights but not feeling right within myself; something was off.

I got severe food poisoning three times. One time, it was so debilitating that I couldn't leave my claustrophobic windowless room in a dirty guesthouse in Thailand for almost two days. A fan blew hot air over my depleted body for hours. I peeled myself off the bed, stumbled down the hall to urinate, and collapsed back into my chamber. No one on the planet knew where I was, and I had no one around to ask for water or help. I was too exhausted to move.

My determined nature didn't allow me to cry uncle and get on the next plane home. I was loyal to my plan to see Asia for nine months, to keep going until I had spent my savings.

I spent more than my savings—by the time I returned to Canada I had spent all of my energy as well. I was depleted. My family doctor, flummoxed after doing every test he could think of—AIDS, parasites, thyroid, and on and on—eventually sent me to the foreign disease specialist at Toronto General Hospital.

Months later, after sending the hospital lots of my pee and poo in tiny plastic bottles, it was time to receive my results from the specialist. *Thank goodness*, I thought. I'm finally going to get a diagnosis so I can fix whatever the problem is and get on with my life.

I waited for hours past my appointment time before I was taken into yet another sterile room. I think this is to offer the illusion that you're somehow closer to seeing the doctor. Eventually, the foreign disease specialist entered with his interns, looking me up and down like the case study I was. He examined the piece of paper he had with my lab results and casually said, "There's nothing wrong with you."

Within two minutes, he both came and went, leaving me in the wake of his cursory visit with a life in ruins. I was devastated. If he's the top guy, the know-it-all-foreign-disease-specialist, then where is there to go from here for answers?

Alone. Unsupported. I looked normal on the outside but I had no energy in my body. I had gone from dancing daily, sometimes up to six or eight hours a day when I was training, to not being able to walk up a flight of stairs. Sapped.

My dream of dancing for a contemporary dance company in England grew dim. I watched my friends continue to perform, choreograph, and join companies while I retired early, before I felt I even got a chance to fly.

Eventually, the label given to my condition was post-viral fatigue syndrome, an autoimmune condition that the foreign disease specialist believed was a result of catching a virus in India that knocked my immune system out. Kaput.

For the next seven-plus years, I struggled with my health. I knew I had to take my healing into my own hands and I was interested in eastern medicine. I began to study Ayurveda and eventually became a Clinical Ayurvedic Specialist.

Ayurveda isn't a quick fix, but it works. It's the art and science of delayed gratification, and that's how I began to heal myself from the debilitating condition that plagued my mind and body for almost a decade.

In my depleted state, I didn't understand all that I was needing to grieve. I had no clue that the loss of my dream to dance was underlying this autoimmune condition. I couldn't see how my loss of innocence and self-esteem were also intertwined in my exhaustion. And I continued to make choices that would take me further and further out of alignment with who I am. But, the universe has a knack for inviting us back to ourselves, no matter how far astray we've gone.

Chapter 12 - My Darkest Teacher

Andrew's death was the portal into the most repulsive experiences and interactions I've ever had to endure.

Death can bring people together or tear them apart. Suicide is such a peculiar way for someone to exit their body—leaving an aftermath of emotion and turmoil, questions and confusion. Especially when that person was the life of the party, the eternal optimist, and everyone's cheerleader.

Shocking doesn't even begin to describe my experience; *devastating* is an understatement.

It was weeks before Andrew's body was found. Every day was an ordeal, a painful waiting, hoping that he would be found…alive. I would shake uncontrollably, my nervous system attempting to deal with the shock of Andrew's disappearance.

What about the family we were planning? What about his son who lived with us part time? What about all of the adventures we had in the making? What about our life…together?

How could this all be gone in a moment?

I was praying for a miracle; I was yearning for my love to come home and everything to be as it was. I was wrestling with life, bargaining with God—anything to have him back.

Instead, I was faced with the stark reality of having to throw out his toothbrush and razor, sort through his material belongings, through every piece of paper he left behind, every book, every shirt, every last piece of his life that was touchable.

The scent of him is still in his clothes and on our bed sheets…his footsteps are imprinted in the carpets…his son's fingerprints are on the windows.

I could still feel him in our home, but he would never return.

The nightmare ensued, not solely because he was gone but because of the hemorrhaging of a family. I never got to say goodbye to my stepson, with whom I had had a strong and loving connection. In-laws were sending me hate mail, verbally threatening my friends, and bullying me. They wanted every last piece of Andrew they could get. I became the scapegoat for them; they had no use for me anymore.

If Andrew had died in a car accident, things might have been different. Maybe. We would have all had to accept that it was an accident.

Suicide is a void. It's vast and bewildering. It can't be blamed on God, so people often look outside themselves to displace their own unresolved remorse. Ugly turns uglier. Luckily, I had a few really enlightened friends and family members who were stable, clear, loving forces. Without them, I probably wouldn't be here.

In the wake of the catastrophe, I was left with paying Andrew's bills, sorting through all his belongings, looking for a new place to live, dealing with the police, and buffering many friends' shock and grief over his death.

Within the following nine months after Andrew was gone, my entire world as I knew it fell apart.

One of my closest friends at the time said things of a very hurtful nature, trying to be helpful I'm sure, but being verbally abusive instead. Totally unconscious or completely oblivious, I'm not sure.

I had to walk away from the only stable yoga teaching contract I had for years after my "friend" and boss lashed out at me at work. Her verbal attack was pernicious. Kicking someone while they are down, grieving, trying to put their life back together, felt truly distasteful.

The universe was forcing me out of any dysfunctional relationship, clearing the path for meaningful and balanced connections, revealing who really had my back and loved me dearly. Fierce grace.

My darkest teacher, loss, sat vigil, present and patient with me when I felt so alone in the world. She amplified my aloneness, turned up the dial on my pain and exposed me to the shadow of all life has to offer. Grief has no timeline. She waited for me, consumed me, ripened me. Sorrow engulfed me so I forgot myself. Suffering was the midwife who carried me from this reality to the next.

Chapter 13 - Life Is Your Initiation

I have been through various initiations in my life: a christening, holy communion, mantra initiation, karma sannyasin initiation, and vision quests. Not to mention numerous ceremonies: graduating from university, sweat lodge ceremonies, women's circles, cord cutting, a wedding, ayahuasca ceremonies, and on and on.

On the spiritual quest of self-improvement, these can be but distractions and glamorous ego-boosting processes to qualify us into some idea of who we are. There may be great merit in these things and I have no regrets, but I see the flimsiness and façade that can be created if the teaching or initiation is not integrated and embodied over time.

I have come to understand; life is my initiation.

There is no need to run off to foreign lands seeking *darshan* (blessing by sight of a holy being) from a two-hundred-year-old enlightened master living in a cave in the Himalayas; unless of course you feel called, which I did, but that's another story. Through various experiences, I discovered that what appeared to be the enlightened person or path was in fact a glorious teacher, but not in the way I thought.

~

"Are you better yet?" a fellow initiate asked, frustrated, one hand on hip, standing righteously in her spiritual orange garb.

"No," I responded with my weak voice as I lay on the wooden ashram bed, feeling pathetic and worthless.

I knew that the ashram had no room or time to support sick people and that if you weren't contributing and doing sixteen hours of karma yoga (selfless service) a day, you would be asked to leave.

I spent my days alone in my bed, shaking with fever, vomiting, having diarrhea and mild hallucinations to round out my ashram stay. I was desperate and began taking other people's medications when they offered them. In my delirious state, the black-market passing out of pills that other foreigners hadn't finished when they had "something just like you had" seemed like a good option.

I pushed myself back into participating in the karma yoga, working tirelessly in the hot sun.

It's embarrassing to admit now but at that time in my life I gave up my power easily to those who I believed had the answers to reaching enlightenment. Looking back I see the irony, living in a place known for preaching spirituality but lacking in compassion and humanity in so many ways.

It took me years to know that I am perfect—that there's nothing I have or will ever do out of alignment with Divine Will. Life will bring me as many initiations as I need. Not as tests, but as opportunities. As I began to see it this way, my suffering diminished and began to dissolve.

I didn't fully know what I was made of until I walked through the fire. True purification leaves no trace of the previous form. If you're in the heat of the fire now in your life, I encourage you to try and soften—get curious about this power that is consuming you.

In my experience, my ego mind kept me feeling separate and held me in a state of suffering. I discovered the key was to befriend my mind and accept whatever came into my consciousness from moment to moment.

I tried not to waste energy pushing away the "negative thoughts." I let them rise on up, acknowledged them, and had compassion for *the one* who was going through the experience (me).

Undone

My heart is unstitching

I've been trying to keep these sutras intact for too many months now.

Again

My heart bleeds open

Spills out across the floor

Messy

Convulsing

Pain seeps out of my third eye into my oatmeal.

This is my life

Alone.

This is where I've been left

To find out it's all not true

To explore the unknown regions of unconditional love

Of Creator's hand, gently on my shoulder

Knowingly, lovingly lifting me up

One stitch at a time

Reminding me I have never

Will never

Come undone.

Chapter 14 - The Space In Between

When you're neither here nor there but you know things will never be the same again... you're in the space in between.

The day, the event, the experience has left an indelible mark somewhere inside you and that changes the way you walk forever. You can't quite locate this mark but you feel it so powerfully within.

Bardo is a Tibetan Buddhist term that refers to the state of existence between death and rebirth. We can experience this state without having to physically die when we're metaphorically, energetically, psychically, cellularly dying and recalibrating before growing into the next version of ourselves.

I found this experience terrifying, beautiful, harrowing, discombobulating, and even welcomed at times.

The death of the old self begins to break down all of the stagnant energies, thoughts, beliefs, and *samskaras*; these are cellular memories and imprints from this life and beyond that will not serve us on our journey moving forward. The time that you spend in the bardo state depends on so many factors, some within your control and some without.

Our conditioning is so ingrained that any change, especially one that we know on a soul level will catapult us upward, can feel like a threat. We hold onto the past. There is trepidation surrounding the unknown. We so often struggle to see beyond our past and what we have already lived and experienced. For me, resistance to this death perpetuated suffering and confusion.

Embracing the dark liminal experience has potential for profound liberation. It's an opportunity to question reality and what is meaningful and vital on our sacred life journey.

I have had a few experiences of walking with death in this lifetime. Physically, in dreamtime, and in ceremony.

One of the initiations I moved through for healing grief was a native plant medicine ceremony with ayahuasca. The room was dark. There were others lying on mats on the floor around the room. Cries, whimpers, and laughter wafted by me and through my body.

I waited to be cleansed, healed in one foul swoop—for something otherworldly to take my anguish away so I could move on with my life. But there was nothing. Twinkling moments of peace and love bookended by excruciating mourning. I lay there for hours, listening to the chanting of the shaman, disconnected and lifeless, succumbing to the inevitable scar this loss would have on me forever.

Then I was called. It was my turn to sit in front of the shaman, so she could sing her song into my heart. As soon as I sat before her, there was a presence, an animal-like energy there. It was black; I could not see her face.

Her voice brought sobs of lamentation from my core. I began to slip away, into the bardo, but this time it was different—this time I yielded.

This time, I allowed myself to die.

I fell into the darkness and I knew I was dying, I knew this is what it's like. I smiled, giddy, fearless. Andrew is okay. I'm okay. It's all okay. Wings grew from my back and I soared, suspended by a soft loving presence—by grace.

This ceremony offered me a visceral experience of death and left an indelible mark on my cells and psyche. It didn't take my pain away indefinitely but it did provide me with some perspective and peace.

Chapter 15 - Spiritual Bullshit

Spiritual bullshit smells the worst. At least with regular bullshit you know what you're looking at and you can use it for fertilizer. Spiritual bullshit is bedazzled and glamorized, covered in *malas* and infused with *Nag Champa*.

I've seen my fair share of it in my time and even unknowingly doled some out myself. I am sure of it. Holy shit reeks. It's pretentious and can be outright damaging to the open-hearted seeker, particularly when offered up by the so-called "enlightened" master.

I know this first hand, as some of my greatest lessons have come as a result of the emotional, psychological, and physical abuse from self-proclaimed "masters" who used their position, power, and spiritual lingo to manipulate, dominate, and confuse.

There is nothing spiritual about these kinds of people.

When I was in my early thirties and married to my first husband, Liam, we returned to Vancouver after living in England. We opened a yoga studio and began the long and arduous Canadian immigration process. This time was very challenging for us. We lived in a tiny cramped space with other people and dying cats, with all of our disposable income going to to the yoga studio.

One afternoon, he called me out of the blue. "I've had an accident..." When his voice came through the phone, I immediately felt sickened. I didn't know it then, but this was the beginning of the end.

Liam accidently cut his finger off ten days before we were to marry and have the grand opening of our yoga studio, something we crazily thought we would do on the same day. I had visions of the accident before it happened, but I didn't want to be the irrational fiancée as he went to his under-the-table carpentry job. So I kept quiet.

Unknowingly, Liam's medical care had expired a few weeks before. We had to pay out of pocket for his surgery. The young surgeon tried desperately to reattach his finger but months later the bone hadn't "taken" and he had his finger amputated.

It's just a finger, you might think, but that finger unlocked the door to an entire lifetime of anger, fear, resentment, frustration, and ultimately depression for my then-husband. Layer upon layer of darkness emerged. I discovered that he would hide away watching porn in our bedroom while I would be giving an Ayurvedic consultation to a client in the next room, trying to keep us afloat financially.

I ignored all sorts of signs and betrayed my own self every time I made excuses for him and hoped things would get better. They didn't.

We decided to sell the yoga studio due to the stress of owning it, and around the same time we came in contact with a very charismatic spiritual teacher. Desperate for purpose, meaning, and spiritual evolution, we clung to this teacher hoping some of his power would rub off on us and that we too would be as enlightened as he claimed to be. Our days were spent with other seekers, sitting in the living room with Master, as he was called, watching him smoke, swear, and share his "wisdom." We were part of his inner circle—the most dangerous place to be.

Spiritual predators prey on the innocent and naive; the desperate, weary, and faithful travelers on the path.

Liam became more entrenched with Master and was told he would travel the world with him and teach alongside this so-called enlightened man. What a perfect complement to Liam's issues of feeling unloved and unrecognized by male figures. Master told Liam that I would have to live in Liam's shadow and I should just suck that up.

Despite being out of work, he began to spend much of his time with Master and came home one day to declare, "I've decided to dedicate my life to Master, above and beyond our marriage."

Fear, panic, grasping, and devastation—it felt like he was having an affair, and one that I couldn't compete with. I would never assuage his daddy issues the way this man would.

I don't care if you're a swami, monk, preacher, yoga teacher, or priest. Nothing gives you the right to use your position of power to manipulate or dominate another human being.

And human beings! You have the responsibility to know yourself and hold your center. Follow what feels expansive and true and right in your body and mind. If it contracts you or makes you feel inferior or devalued, it's not the path of enlightenment. No one can take your power or energy from you unless you allow it on some level—I learned this the hard way.

I so desperately wanted the Creator to notice me and think I was special, so I gave up parts of myself and ignored my inner guidance in lieu of spiritual ideals and beliefs.

The irony was lost on me for years.

Now I know.

Anytime you give your power away to another, you weaken your immune system and your nervous system and you lower your self-esteem. Unfortunately there are many teachers, leaders, and gurus who feed off the energy that others give when followers look up to them, emulate them, or put them on a pedestal.

This level of manipulation (even on a subtle level) works to control and maintain a hierarchy. In the yogic lineage I followed for many years, this mentality always kept you "less than"—a constant reminder that the guru is the enlightened one and that his level of consciousness isn't available to anyone else in this lifetime.

I call bullshit. Spiritual bullshit.

It was this perverse mentality that I allowed to seep into my nervous system and psyche and overtake me with an autoimmune *dis-ease* for over seven years. The root of this condition was giving away my power, believing someone else knew what was better for me, and never accessing my divine nature unless I was blessed by the guru to do so.

I didn't see this at the time; only years later was I able to unravel the complex threads of entrapment of my spirit, cloaked in a spiritual lineage and philosophy that is broken at its foundation and perpetuates more broken, dependent people in the false name of spirituality.

Through my experiences I have come to know that it is my *dharma* to inspire others to bask in self-sovereignty, a form of self-empowerment that is rooted in depth, self-knowing, and holding one's center as close as possible to truth.

If you find yourself at the feet of a guru or enamored with a great teacher, that's okay, that's part of your journey. Just don't give up your own heart and inner knowing of what's true for you.

I have come to know, we are all Divine.

We are not separate—never have been, never will be—from the very Source from which we came. There is no-thing we could do, create, or experience to evict us from the love that is the essence of who we are and what we came to remember.

Chapter 16 - Hospitalized

Slippers covered the feet shuffling along the tile floor of the hospital. A body, bones, and flesh being corralled along with an intravenous cord attached, toward the room. Drip, drip, dripping…each precious nectar of saline solution filled this bag of bones that hung as though it had weathered hundreds of winters.

It was my body.

How could this be *my* body?

I've had so many bodies in this one lifetime…so many versions of this flesh…never the same from day to day. This body has betrayed me relentlessly but always rebounds: a seven-year illness after my fateful trip to India; a mysterious inflammation of my face and neck until I was unrecognizable; blistering hands erupting every time I attempt to holiday in a tropical climate; a growth on my leg that left me on crutches as I hobbled across the stage to receive my university degree in contemporary dance; and on.

As I lay in the windowless room, surrounded by the gray walls of a third-world hospital, I felt both resignation and peace. The combination felt like *surrender.* The irony is that surrender was the word I had chosen for this two-and-a-half-month journey to Bali. Silly me, I should have chosen fun.

I know now that surrender isn't an intellectual exercise or a cliché that yoga teachers spout out (because that's what we're supposed to say, right?). Surrender is a process of awakening. It's the face of grace that initially stings, like when the nurse stabs around and ruptures five veins before finding the one that will freely give blood. But once it's in, it's in.

Once surrender has happened, it can't un-happen, because something in us has changed. Died. Transformed. Transmuted.

I'm not good at surrendering, but I'm getting lots of practice. What started out as a just-like-the-bout-in-India diarrhea ended up transpiring into a month of not being able to keep food down and eventually leading to hospitalization. But, what happened in those five days, hooked up to an IV in a hospital in Bali, was much more than salmonella gone bad. It was an initiation. And every initiation is about crossing a line and expanding into the next realm of possibility.

Not all initiations have to be as shitty (literally) as mine. Yours may feel more subtle, soft, and graceful—or, more severe, dramatic, and harsh. It doesn't matter. My way is my way and your way is yours.

In the surrender, I swallowed life whole—the sacred, the disgusting, and the *all that is*. When I'm willing to embrace the whole of life, this is my freedom. I say I want it all, but do I? Wanting it all means the dark and the light. Most of my life I ran from the dark, avoiding it as if it had no value, nothing to teach me.

Experience has taught me there is so much wisdom in the darkness, in the night, in the stillness, in the wintertime of life. I had to turn and face what was most uncomfortable to look at and be with: my anger, impatience, self-denial, depression, anxiety, and blame.

These fragmented aspects of myself needed acknowledgement and love too.

The self-improvement industry thrives on a society that thinks it needs to be better, do better, do more, and be more. A deep scarcity-and-lack mentality eroded me from inside, and so much energy was spent on the incessant quest for more, better, more, better...

What if the real quest were one of radical self-acceptance and self-love?

Surrender Leads to Trust

Surrender Leads to Trust

(It's not the other way around.)

Surrender when you're blindsided by life.

Surrender when you can't hold it anymore.

Surrender when you're ready to dance with your demons.

Surrender when it's all been taken from you.

Surrender when the incomprehensible has moved into your life.

Surrender when you don't know who the hell you are anymore.

Surrender when it doesn't make sense.

Surrender when it's so bloody perfect that you've stopped
questioning right or wrong.

Surrender when love of this ecstatic life shreds you apart, rips you
open, and shows you who you really are.

And at the end of it, don't ask, "Who am I now?"

Instead, sit in the quiet knowing that it never really mattered.

Go live your glorious, treacherous, ever-expanding life.

Chapter 17 - Forgiveness

Forgiveness: you can't rush it and you can't fake it.

It's no secret that holding onto resentment, blame, criticism, and judgment will eat away at our insides and make us bitter, sick, or both. Perhaps there's another way. Sick and bitter lead us in the opposite direction of freedom. Forgiveness, on the other hand, is guaranteed to lead you in the direction of liberation. And there is a formula for it.

One part acceptance. (That's where you see things are they are).

One part willingness. (That's where you get busy and do something productive).

One part grace. (That's where you trust that there are some things best left to a higher power).

Acceptance does not mean condoning or saying that something was okay when it wasn't. It doesn't mean that the hurt, abuse, pain, or betrayal endured was valid or just. Acceptance means acknowledging that an event or experience transpired, and that you're ready to see it for what it was and move beyond the pain of it. It means you are ready to release yourself from that which has been holding your life force hostage. Acceptance is no longer letting a person or event consume any more of your psychic real estate.

Take whatever time you need to be in your anger or frustration or blame, and when you are ready (and only when you are ready), reclaim your wholeness and take responsibility for your response to whatever happened; this is the vestibule of forgiveness.

What is...is.

There must be willingness to accept. We don't need to pretend or rush acceptance. Take whatever time you need to be in your anger or frustration or blame, just don't stay there eternally. Make a commitment to yourself that you will move beyond. No. Matter. What.

As contradictory as this may sound, I found that the darkness was so unbearable that it became the polar tension that catapulted me beyond my life situation and back into the remembrance of my truth—that I am Divine. I was determined to find a way through the pain.

I realized that when I would perceive a person, event, or situation that was holding me hostage as something that ruined my life, broke, or tainted me, then I was giving my power away. This person or event has assisted in making me who I am, and has added to the incredible tapestry of my life experiences. What I do with it is up to me.

It took me a long time to be ready and willing to forgive my first husband, Liam. I feel that's because of the degree to which I gave my power away to him. I was so used to giving my power away by doing everything I thought he wanted me to and then feeling resentful when he wasn't responding how I expected. This blame cycle got in the way of me taking responsibility for my life as well as freeing myself through forgiveness.

Forgiveness is the ultimate act of liberating yourself from your past.

Forgiveness will literally transform your cellular memory, dissolve the toxic residue that accumulates in your mind-body from holding onto resentment, and free your energy body of the need to manifest as illness in the physical. The lack of forgiveness and absolution leads to dis-ease, robbing you of your natural vital flow of pranic life force and distorting your perception of reality.

Finding peace with what is and what has been allows the body to heal and release any stored mental and emotional pain. I will offer you tools and mindfulness-based practices in Part Three of this book.

Deep Bows of Gratitude

Deep bows of gratitude to those souls who have built me up by tearing me down,

who have tested my character and enhanced my resilience and tenacity.

Deep bows of gratitude to those who have done the unspeakable,

who have given me the opportunity to remember the truth of who I am,

I am light and no-thing can destroy my spirit.

No-thing can ruin me.

I am a child of God.

I am whole and complete and you can never take that from me.

Chapter 18 - Life Dismantled

It wasn't until long after Andrew died that I realized, I can't get my life wrong. I can't even make a mistake. Even through the most testing times when it looks like everything is falling apart, I now believe that new life will spring forth.

The Divine didn't take the very things I loved away to punish me. If only I could have seen the entirety of my life at the time, the whole vision, I would understand why the challenges and losses were crucial to my awakening back into wholeness and love.

I could only see the present moment; my life circumstances and the awful future I was projecting for myself.

On a deeper level, my soul knew my potential and danced with life to wake me up to it, to get me on board with the spectacular possibilities for my life's experience and expression. It was a process and took time before I began to see my life from this perspective.

I've noticed that most people don't wake up through the cushy times. In the midst of turmoil, some of us are compelled to ascend; or, once the storms have passed and we have time to reflect. For me I knew that if I didn't proactively rise up, I would be swallowed.

The innate desire humans have for expansion is the fierceness required to transcend our previously limiting ideas and beliefs about ourselves, the world, and our relationship to all things. My life needed to be dismantled to be resurrected. Otherwise I likely would have kept dragging around thoughts, emotions, and ways of being that were no longer in resonance with the version of myself that knew I was already whole.

In Hindu mythology, the Goddess Kali is the goddess of death, destruction, and time. She is fierce and ruthless. Her name literally means "black night." Kali is the energy that arrives in our life to shake out all the things that are not of us.

At times I went kicking and screaming (and thus endured more suffering), and other times I honored this force and her wisdom. Interestingly, Kali is also symbolic of motherly love. The most enlightened form of grace is harsh when necessary, but she is always working with loving intention to uplift our life.

Kali came to me in the form of unthinkable loss. She helped to clarify who I wanted to be, how I wanted to spend my time on earth, and who I wanted to spend it with.

When Kali comes calling she will tear your life apart, make it unrecognizable, *and* be there to soothe your tender heart when you're left bawling your eyes out on the bathroom floor. I lost friends, my community, a job—everything that no longer was in vibrational alignment with the new version of myself that was emerging. I had to give up being a pleaser, not valuing myself or my gifts, having weak boundaries, and hanging out with manipulative people.

I had to trust I was on *my* path despite the destruction. The path is not always comfortable.

In this life we all have a unique journey and there's no right or wrong way to do it. Get curious about the conditions in your life that displease you. Give yourself permission to feel them and know you are not your life situation. It does not define you unless you allow it to.

If you find yourself in the wintertime of your life—meeting loss, death, grief, or suffering—know this inward time of isolation, living in the abyss and despairing, are the natural precursors to spring. All of the seasons have their particular exquisiteness and intensity. You can't always be in the summertime of your life. Knowing this and relaxing into the natural rhythms can soften the resistance that often arises in the darkness.

Chapter 19 - Death of the Self

Destruction Precedes Creation

Through perilous times, I felt like I was literally dying. My identity was annihilated, my cells were restructuring, and my surroundings were taken from me. I changed in unrecognizable ways—both internally and externally. The way I related to the world and perceived it was destroyed. This happened both in an instant and, simultaneously, slowly over time.

This journey was frightening and discombobulating. Without an understanding of this process, the nature of the Self being demolished, one can find oneself breaking down.

With a strong spiritual foundation and a stable nervous system already intact, this development is a natural breakthrough and a breaking away from all of our karmic ties, our energetic mental and emotional stagnation, and a sense of Self that will not serve us on the next leg of our journey.

I died without dying.

I kept this body, yet internally I was transformed. My nervous system was rewired. My hard drive was wiped clean. I got a new crack at life!

This sounds a little creepy; however, it's one of the most exquisite metamorphosis we can experience without having to leave this body.

This didn't come without its own set of challenges and work, without me needing to reorient myself. I experienced memory loss, I felt like I didn't know anything, I wasn't able to find my words, I lost track of time and space; it felt overwhelming. This worked its way through in time, as I adjusted.

Like a baby learning how to maneuver in this realm, I had to learn a new way of being. The wonder of this is that it was up to me to consciously rewire my neuropathways to have a new experience of my life. We get to decide who we want to be, how we want to feel, and what we will make things mean in our reality. We always had this choice and capability; however, we didn't always exercise this opportunity in the most expansive way.

After having an autoimmune condition for over seven years, I adopted a belief that I didn't have energy and wasn't physically very strong anymore. I knew I needed to confront this false belief and rewire the pathways in my brain that connected my sense of self with lacking energy. My adventure to the Grand Teton in Wyoming was one of these experiences in which I broke the barrier of my own belief and proved to myself the fabrication I had been living by...

The Yoga of Faith

Silent.

Hovering.

Floating through the air at 5 a.m, slivers of light piercing the cumulus and reaching my skin.

I wondered...*How do we actually fly? How are we really being propelled through the sky in this tiny piece of metal?*

I sat in the back of the bitty four-seater Bonanza, a tiny plane only two years older than me. I had been invited on a journey to climb the Grand Teton, one of North America's most iconic mountains.

Mick, our guide, connected his iPod to the plane's circuitry and through my headphones played John Denver's "Leaving on a Jet Plane." How appropriate.

And simultaneously, somewhere in my psyche, the thought passed through me, *Am I going to die on this trip?*

What I didn't realize then was that yes…a part of me would.

Flying has always been a mystical experience for me. I enter the *bardo*—the place in between worlds—neither here nor there, looking down upon the landscape and seeing it from a perspective that many will never have the opportunity to see. As we pierced through the clouds, Mount Rainier seared its beauty into the gray matter of my brain so I would never forget its majesty, presence, and healing power.

Four hours later we landed on a teeny landing strip in Jackson Hole, Wyoming. Peter (our third team member and pilot), Mick and I ate some lunch at the Lotus Café before heading to the grocery store to purchase our supplies for the next three nights when we would be camping in the mountains. Weight is always a consideration—whatever we're taking in, we have to carry up and out.

There is a fine art to packing a backpack for a climbing trip; this is an art form I am not versed in at all. All I know is that you're only allowed one pair of underwear for four days in the mountains—at least that's Mick's rule.

We reached camp by dark, hung up our food so the bears wouldn't be tempted, set up our tent, and went to bed. Unfortunately sharing a tent with two snoring men and falling asleep isn't copacetic with me. Needless to say, I didn't get much sleep.

The next day we arrived at the extremely rocky base camp. It was like a minefield of stone rubble everywhere—much too high for any vegetation to grow.

Hours later we would awaken in the darkness to begin our ascent. What I didn't fully realize at the time was that this journey was more about going inwards than upwards.

Nothing prepares you for certain life-changing experiences. Granted, I had probably not done the adequate physical training to attempt this climb, but my determination made up for my lack of solid physical preparation.

I also hadn't done much research about the area or what to expect. Sometimes I go with the flow too much—what I hadn't realized is that we were going to be rock climbing up the mountain, not just hiking.

At our base camp at 10,900 feet, I could already feel the effects of altitude: harder to breathe and walk, slight headache, and nausea.

We climbed in the early hours of the morning until the slightest fraction of daylight began to wake up the sky. The crest of the moon hung like an emblem of hope and inspiration. We trudged onwards, across some slick ice, before beginning to rock climb up and up and up.

I'm a relatively new climber. I would consider myself a beginner with perhaps some natural inclination for how to move across a rock face. I don't feel comfortable on exposed pieces of sheer rock, dangling like a flimsy piece of flesh thousands of feet above the ground.

Vulnerable. Exposed. Insignificant.

One pitch after another we climbed. There were moves that seemed impossible to me. I couldn't comprehend how I could go any higher. I didn't see anything to hold onto or grab, but when I would peer down I would see Peter, my climbing partner, coming up behind me and I knew I had to keep moving. If I slipped or fell, I could totally take Peter out. If he fell, he could pull me down with him.

I had to keep moving. Quitting wasn't an option.

The breath saved me. Exhaling forcefully to ground and center myself, as well as to help with the increasing altitude, was my lifeline. Hour after hour we carried on upwards toward the elusive summit. The sun was intense—I was thirsty, hungry, and tired.

The higher we climbed and the more fatigued I felt, the more acute the demons within my mind became. Fear, grief, anger, and doubt all moved through me. I offered these hellions to the rock, like a sacred gift—the only thing I had left to give to the Divine.

What remained was gratitude, peace, and acceptance of all my life's hardships and challenges.

The mountains stood silent...willing...strong...without judgment. I was both held lovingly and asked to push beyond who I thought I was and what I thought I could accomplish.

As I continued to move, I could feel the reprogramming of who I was and who I believed myself to be. I consciously released the doubt and fear from my cells as I recognized that I was capable of reaching the summit.

I shifted into the mindset of abundance.

Instead of focusing on the lack of energy, strength, water, and food that I felt I was deficient in at the time, I began to see that I was totally taken care of, that only having one cup of water left before even reaching the summit was all I needed, that despite feeling exhausted I did have all the energy I needed.

I softened into acceptance and faith instead of trying to control the situation (which was futile anyway) and I let life guide me.

For me, the rollercoaster of excitement and anticipation through the phases of hard work and determination moved into doubt and fatigue, escalated into grief, loss, and anger, which in turn opened the doorways for forgiveness and acceptance before I even got to the summit.

Moments of utter bliss and exuberance filled me also. I dangled from a thread over sheer nothingness—the ground thousands of feet below me. The beauty was astounding and awe inspiring. I didn't know if it was the view or the altitude that took my breath away.

Throughout the hours that made up the summit day, I encountered every emotion. My cells were wrung out, cleansed, and rebooted. Faith was my lifeline. Knowing that whatever happened was okay brought me solace. Transformation isn't linear or pretty or stable or guaranteed.

Arriving at the summit was profoundly fantastic but somewhat anticlimactic compared with the inner journey I had been on. Little did I know that the descent would challenge me too. We had no water left. All I had eaten in the previous twelve hours had been power bars, peanut butter sandwiches, Reese's Pieces, and trail mix, which really put a damper on my usual Ayurvedically-appropriate food choices. I had pains in my stomach, perhaps from the altitude but more likely from the dry foods. Fatigue and dehydration overwhelmed me.

Down climbing is treacherous on the knees and there was so much scree that I fell on my ass thrice. Mick kindly offered to carry my backpack for me and I thought, No way. This is the only padding I have for when I topple over. I stumbled back to our rocky base camp and lay down in the tent. My head was pounding from the altitude and dehydration; I had to hold my skull in my hands to relieve the tension.

Peter quickly made ramen noodles and delivered them to the tent door. They were the best ramen noodles I had ever tasted. I was so touched by his care and so full of gratitude, despite my inner voice telling me how pathetic I was not to be a fully functioning human at that point in time. Advil is a beautiful thing…I took two extra strength capsules at once. That may have been one of the best decisions I've ever made.

Throughout the dark night, I could see other climbers in the distance walking along the trail with their headlamps on—going up, coming down.

In the morning, the sun broke the sky open, sending light flashing onto the Middle Teton, reminding me how lucky I was to be alive and having this awesome human experience.

After having to skillfully poo into a tiny silver bag, I strapped it to the outside of my backpack before beginning our four-hour hike out of the mountains. The sun was blazing. We hiked from the rocky terrain eventually back to a level where vegetation could grow, into lush meadows with mountain streams running through, and then into the dry forest landscape where we had begun. I fantasized about what I would eat at the Lotus Café back in Jackson Hole once we got down. I imagined what it would feel like to have a shower and put on clean clothes, even though it would be the next day before that actually happened.

Flying back to Seattle in the little four-seater Bonanza was quiet and peaceful. The Dream Team had bonded and succeeded together. But it struck me that even if we hadn't made it to the summit of the Grand Teton, our trip would still have been a huge success. Metamorphosis is about the quality of life moving through you during the journey, because in life we only spend a few moments at the summit.

We get to the top, eat some potato chips, take some photos, and leave. Proportionally, being at the top is a fleeting moment compared with the journey it took to get there.

I realized that life is now. I questioned how I was living mine.

I recognized that if I allow it, I will die over and over again in this life or, more accurately put, I will be reborn time and time again. This is magnificent—I'm not trapped by any outdated version of myself, I'm not confined by my past. The power is within me to transcend who I thought I was and become the person I truly want to be.

Petrichor

You know

there's a word for the smell in the air

outside

after it rains.

That scent so full of life

bursting forth

making childlike wonders

in my heart.

I never knew

that the earth

releases an oil into the air

before the rain even falls.

Anticipating,

marking this transition,

as the storm is brewing,

knowing there will be

an after.

Chapter 20 - How About a Miracle?

I need a miracle. Please. God, bring me a miracle. Take my pain away.

In unspeakable times I wished that the hand of Grace would swoop down and soothe my sorrows, but the Creator knew better than to rob me of these intense moments that propelled me into a more compassionate, strengthened version of myself.

In the book *A Course in Miracles*, a miracle is defined as a shift in perception from fear to love. At first I thought this was such a letdown. I want angels! And bright lights and a big-deal-kinda-miracle.

However, the experience of traversing through life with this attitude at the helm is extraordinary, because it means every single one of us has the capacity to transform our very thoughts that are the illusive barrier between perceiving reality through the wounded ego's fear-based lens or through the Divine lens of love.

If you would prefer to be a cynic or remain bitter, this is your prerogative. But I assure you, choosing to see life from the viewpoint of love feels so much better. So why not? Would you rather be righteous and hold onto a position for months, years, or decades?

We have the power to release ourselves from our own shackles. You can emancipate yourself from the slave you have become to your own thoughts and beliefs. You are the miracle you're seeking. Freedom is only a thought away.

So why is it so inconvenient and onerous to see life and other people (especially the really annoying, naughty, belligerent ones) the way Source does?

We've been conditioned from our youth to discern via a dualistic vantage point: up-down, right-wrong, day-night, happy-sad. This is how this three-dimensional reality works; however, this can also cause a lot of continued suffering as we're often comparing one thing to another or fighting against what is.

Miracles aren't so fussy. Love has a boundless capacity for infinite inclusion. We all do. Learning to see through the eyes of love opposed to fear is a skill that we can all brush up on. Understanding that every single person makes the best decision they can from the level of consciousness they are operating from at any given moment allows us to see that everyone truly is doing the best they can, even if it's not what we like or want. Yourself included.

I used to lament about past decisions. "I wish I would have known what I know now." Well, I didn't. I couldn't have. And it's perfectly okay that what happened, happened.

I've learned to place my attention on how I want to move forward, instead of focusing on the past. I ask myself how I want to show up in my life now. I get to choose if I continue to see through the eyes of fear and live with ongoing blame, impatience, anger, frustration, doubt, depression, or regret.

These are all glaring signs that fear is the modus operandi.

Love is not pushy, anxious, forceful, or needy. When I hear the voice in my head tainted with any of these tones, I know it's the wounded ego attempting to keep me "safe." The wounded ego's idea of keeping me safe translates to continuous affliction.

Sure, I've got lots of proof that life has done me wrong, people have betrayed me, and I was handed a shitty deal. But can I really know this for a fact? Can I fully understand why my life has been the way it has? What if there were a much larger view that spans lifetimes? What if my soul has a lot more choice about what it wants to experience in this human body than I ever knew?

What if everything is going perfectly according to the plan?

What if life is happening, and we get to choose how we co-create with life by how we decide to feel and respond to what life brings us? I now realize that I get to choose how I think, feel, and respond to everything. This includes Andrew taking his own life.

I believe there is much more freedom in trusting in an intelligence greater than my individual self. The same energy that created us is also taking care of us; if only we could see it that way without comparing our life to someone else's.

Surrendering to the miracles all around helped me heal. I decided to see as the Creator may see—that no one or no-thing is out of place, wrong, or lacking for the exact purpose and desired outcome individually and collectively.

Chapter 21 - We Are a Microcosm of the Macrocosm

We are a microcosm of the macrocosm. We are infinite and eternal.

The power that brought us here will take us away, and that same benevolent force sustains us whilst we are gracing this planet. How could it be any other way? We are each a drop of water in the ocean of consciousness. We are *that*.

It took me years to understand that I need not fight against life or others. I need not defend myself to the one who created me. I turned to face the light, to face myself, to face the truth. When I feel love in the form of my breath as it comes in and out, it asks nothing from me. Life asks nothing from me—yet gives me everything I need.

How do you know you don't need it? "You don't have it," as spiritual teacher Byron Katie would say. I have found so much solace in the belief that I have everything I need at any given time, even if I'm uncomfortable or wanting something very different.

My life doesn't look the way I thought it would.

I expect yours doesn't either.

Ask almost anyone and you will find a human who has lost and who has made it through one hundred percent of their life challenges. I'm a forty-one-year-old divorcee and widow. And I'm so much more than these things, these experiences. I'm a soul on an incredible journey, just like you. I've never felt so strong and whole—and so raw and vulnerable.

I've learned that there's room for all of it in my life. I welcome the whole of me and the entirety of my life's experiences. I see value and blessings in all of it. I choose to look back only to propel me forward and to be reminded of the delicacy and impermanence of this precious life.

Wake up. Wake up now. It's time. You are a child of the Creator and there is joy waiting for you. Your eternal nature abides within and will quietly wait to be remembered. Wake up to the miracle you are…we are…IT is.

Give up what no longer serves your highest good so you can focus on what does.

Chapter 22 - Life After Loss

I'm so sorry for your loss and the wretched pain you've endured.

Part of me wishes I could take away all your agony and protect you from the disappointment, betrayal, frustration, rage, grief, terror, and the venomous experiences you've been through. But I won't steal them from you—instead, I'll honor you. I'll celebrate you and your life's journey.

I know you are a phoenix and you will transmute the destructive energies that befriended you for a leg of your sojourn, however long that may take. I believe that nothing can ever or will ever destroy your Spirit.

You are timeless, limitless, omnipotent.

When the veils become so laden and dense that it's impossible to remember who you truly are…soften. Let your heart break open and be still.

Oblige life's desire to wake you up to your magnificence.

This is where you're going anyway—back home. Home to the beating heart and pulsing life at your fingertips, the genius mind living through you as Divinity, the extraordinary experience through time and space that you chose. You decided to be here…so be here. Fully.

Be present to the triumphs and innermost sorrows; there is life and wisdom waiting for you wherever you find yourself and however you find yourself. Waste no more time judging, defending, or lamenting than you need. And by all means take the time you need, just not one moment more. Let your suffering be crystallized into an amulet of grace.

Pour yourself into the task of truth seeing, of seeking out the benevolence and beauty of it all. Go out of your way to ruminate on the jewels and wonders of your odyssey.

Why not?

Why not choose to appreciate the time you've got here, the people who *do* love you, and all that you have and are by your very nature?

You are a vagabond held in the heart of the Divine Mother. You will never be left alone, denied, or refused. Go to Her—she is waiting. She is closer than you think, She lives within your very heart. Silently, tenderly, and eternally.

Chapter 23 - Accepting Impermanence

We know cognitively that everything is in constant flux and will never be what it once was. Everything is changing; nothing is permanent. Yet, we live like we have all the time in the world, not fully showing up for ourselves as ourselves in the truest and most complete expression.

We must stop living a half-life—stop holding onto past resentments or frustrations or situations we cannot change if we want a different experience of reality.

Go live your life. Do what you've always wanted to do and, most importantly, be who you came here to be.

What you believe was an end is a portal to a new beginning. Tomorrow may never come and even if it does, you most definitely want to be the splendid, whole, Divine Self that you are.

There will never be another you. There will never be another today.

This. Is. A. Miracle.

You are a miracle.

PART 3:
My Tools

Chapter 24 - Grief Sucks

Grief is powerful. Grief has a force and life all its own. We can't arm wrestle grief or use sneaky ninja moves to bamboozle it. Grief will devour us and bring us to our knees. We must let it.

A foolish and cowardly man will run from mourning and even feel he has outsmarted it. Drugs, alcohol, sex, overworking, food, depression—you name it. Each of these distractions can provide us with a lacquer finish for our grief that will seal it in so tightly that it may be covered up for years.

This may be a good thing (our subconscious is very intelligent) but it's not a solution. Our pain will always be waiting for us to return home to see what we've left in the tickle trunk of our heart.

Our culture has a twisted relationship with sorrow. Through my experiences I've found that many people don't know how to deal with it or support someone they love moving through this process. In other cultures there are ceremonies, traditions, and a strong sense of community coming together to support the one in mourning.

Your calamity may be different from mine—you may have been through a divorce, had your children grow up and move away, witnessed your parent pass on, lost a job, had a pet die, been forced to move, had cancer, or awakened to the loss of your own innocence and youth. Whatever it is, don't minimize it or dismiss it, and don't over indulge or dramatize it either.

Let your grief be true to you.

In my experience, it's not a linear, rational process we can walk through, check the boxes off, and move on. It's just not like that.

You are unique, and this initiation is yours to navigate in a way that feels most authentic and honoring of who you are. Don't let others dictate how to grieve.

Initially after Andrew's death, there was a lot of support: people bringing food and flowers, phoning, texting; a friend even began a collection from the yoga community to assist me financially.

I am forever grateful for every prayer and act of kindness and love sent my way.

But it seems that we need some grief education, both for the one grieving and for the one trying to support. Here are some insights and suggestions from my experience but please find what feels right for you, as each of us is inimitable and needs something different.

There Is No Right or Wrong Way to Grieve

Nobody knows how it feels to be going through what you're going through. You can't do grieving wrong.

I had a friend who wanted to micromanage my grief and anger after my beloved's death. She tried to get me to "shake it out" and told me that I needed to be grateful for the life I had; she didn't care if she made me cry. She thought that the tough-love card would somehow snap me out of it.

This was traumatic in itself.

I felt humiliated by her comments. For the first time in my life, I knew how it felt to want to kill myself. I felt like I was a burden and that I wasn't loved and accepted unless I was happy. The underlying message I received was:

How you're grieving is making me really uncomfortable and I wish you would hurry up and get back to how you were before you lost your partner so that I can feel better and know how to relate to you.

Don't let anyone tell you, overtly or covertly, that you're somehow not up to snuff in the lamentation department.

She told me she just didn't know how to support me and that I was too sensitive to which I responded, "Why don't you ask how you could support me?"

It's as simple as that.

Yes, it's terribly uncomfortable to both witness and be witnessed in pain, but don't let anyone steal your process from you. If they can't handle it, they shouldn't be there. If you've recently gone through deep loss, you may not be able to articulate what you need or you may be too exhausted to do so. This is not the time to worry about others; give yourself permission to be however you are.

You may not even know how you need support. Give yourself a lot of space for not knowing to be okay. If you do know what support would look or feel like, ask. Perhaps you need someone to just sit quietly and be with you. Or, maybe having a loved one listen to your story over and over again feels beneficial.

Give Yourself Permission to Be Messy

It's not going to be pretty. Grief doesn't want to be pretty. Grief may want to tear you apart to expose your heart and soul to the delicate nature of life and rub your face in the dirt while you're down there, just to be sure. Just to be sure that you have an opportunity to fully love yourself when you're out the other side. Then you'll know why it's so important to wake up to reality—to make it your life's mission to love and accept yourself and know the Divine presence every damn day of your life once you've surfaced from this abject initiation.

Allow yourself to break open. Let your core be exposed to the air, to the shadow, and to the light. Raw. Exposed. Vulnerable. Feel every ounce of the wretched pain in your breath, your heart, your connective tissue… let it seep into your bones. You can't analyze your way through loss and grief; you must feel your way through.

At times, the pain will feel unbearable; it will consume you, it will kill you. And then you will wake, a new day, and there will be a sliver of relief before you are tossed back into the inferno.

This repetitive hell is tapas—you can let it destroy you or, heal you. Tapas is the fiery discipline that purifies your heart and soul.

It is the path of awakening through grief.

It is the most treacherous and lonely of paths. It is the initiation that will return you to Source, to the Creator, to the essence of who and what you are… but not quickly. It will take longer than you think you can bear. It may test your willingness to be here on this planet and take you to the edge of the life you knew before.

Life will never be the same again.

Weep on the bathroom floor. Let your eyes burn from the tears crudely streaming down your cheeks. Curse, scream, and wail until your throat is dry and hoarse. Dance the anguish through your veins if you can, sing your sorrow, or let others sing it for you. Experience the agony of losing the very thing you loved the most and thought you could never live without. Feel the tragedy of not wanting to go on, of seeing no point, of feeling so desperate and dead inside in your isolated place, of no one really able to understand what you're going through, because they can't. They can't. They really can't.

At some point you realize you are utterly alone on this journey. Deserted, despite people being around you. Abandoned to the abyss. This is where Source meets you—in your unaccompanied state where there is no one and nowhere to seek refuge. She cannot meet you when you won't allow her in. She will enter through your agony and torment, so don't rush this part of the initiation.

Loss is inevitable in this lifetime; it's a done deal. You can resist change and impermanence if you choose…this is the road to suffering.

Don't Let Anyone Rush You through the Grieving Process

Give yourself permission for it to take the time it takes—don't let anyone rush you through the grieving process.

What I hated the most, especially in the weeks and months following my loss was the clichéd response that it will "just take time." I wanted to say fuck you to every person who threw this pithy and pathetic line at me.

Clearly, they didn't know that time was my enemy.

Every moment of every day felt like an eternity that I had to endure, moment after moment of hellish thoughts with no respite. My body was in agony from the stress and I couldn't sleep. I took sleeping pills to put me under for about five hours a night, but often I entered another hell in my dream space as my subconscious mind detoxified. It was hell to be awake or asleep.

The world may want to rush you through it. Friends may stop inviting you to things or including you, or they may avoid asking you about your grief completely so that they aren't the ones to "bring it up."

Bring it up? Are you kidding me? Like I had forgotten…like you mentioning my loss would be the reminder that it happened!

Don't be afraid to ask and give lots of space for the person grieving to choose to talk about it or not. In my case, many people wanted to know what happened to Andrew. Some people were curious from a distance; they wanted to know but didn't care enough to reach out to me personally. Many were curious and cared. I lost so much of my life force telling the story over and over. Even to this day, I give myself permission to talk about my loss or not, because I know the effects that talking about it has on my nervous system.

Honor yourself. You don't owe anyone an explanation. Your true friends will understand this. Ironically, they will also be the ones you will naturally want to share with.

Truth is exposed in the rawness of tragedy.

Surround Yourself with People Who Truly Have Your Best Interest at Heart

The people you least expect will rise, rise, rise, and some of your closest kin may drop you in an instant or stab you in the back.

This has nothing to do with you.

Focus on who has come to walk the treacherous path with you; these are your angels in human disguise.

A friend whom I was just getting to know when Andrew died rose to meet the pain of my heart as though she was sent by some higher force to keep me alive. She came and spent nights with me at my apartment; she rubbed my feet to help me sleep at night; she drove me around in her car when I had to look for a new place to live.

Family came to stay with me, friends brought take-out, and others helped in the painstaking process to sort through Andrew's material belongings. One friend drove up to Vancouver and back from the United States in a day to give me an Ayurvedic massage and cook a wholesome meal for me.

Align with those who care about your life. Be open to support from places you may not have expected.

Say No to Anything and Anyone Who Is Causing You More Pain

People I thought I could trust or rely on disappeared. I was made the scapegoat in the midst of tragedy. Few wanted to stick around

through the mess and heartache of putting my life back together.

Extended family members and friends intentionally and unintentionally caused me further suffering. Hurt people hurt people. This I experienced in my rawness and vulnerability. I pray this is not your trip but, if it is, I understand how excruciating this process is. Disconnect from anyone and anything that is causing you more heartache.

Your own past unresolved issues will float to the surface, like air bubbles in water needing to pop. This is time for deep house cleaning; it's not a choice. It just happens if you let it...please let it.

Supporting a Loved One

If you are the one supporting a loved one who is grieving, make specific offers for how you will help without any expectation. For example, make dinner for your loved one and tell them you will bring it over on Thursday at 5 p.m. and will just leave it at the door if they don't want any company at that time.

There is nothing to fix, so no need to rush in and try and soothe things with platitudes like, "Things will get better with time," "This is what God wanted," "It's all for the best," "Cheer up; you've got so much to be happy for," "Count your blessings," and the like.

Just be present with your friend. Listen with a sense of curiosity and an open heart without clouding the moment with your own discomfort around the situation. Allow them to be witnessed in their sorrow, no matter how painful that may be. Have compassion for your friend's loss and patience as you hold their heart tenderly; one day, you may be in their position.

Get Support

Support will look and feel how you need it to look and feel. It may be counseling, energy work, or seeing a psychologist or someone you trust. Make sure you have faith in those you seek from.

At the height of your trauma, it may be hard to trust many people. Everything may feel scary, surreal, and threatening. It's important to be witnessed in your grief and have your sorrow honored. You will do much of your mourning alone, yes. But there must be acknowledgment by trusted companions that you are moving through an excruciating time, and they can still witness you as whole. Find those who can hold this space for you.

I went to one well-intentioned counselor who said what I was going through was normal. This was the last thing I wanted to hear. I didn't want to be lumped in that category. I didn't want to be another statistic, a victim of suicide going through the five stages of grief. I wanted an answer. I wanted someone who knew what the hell was happening, someone who had walked through the fire and come out the other side.

I decided to do things differently. I've always gravitated toward the unorthodox and unusual to pioneer my own way. This is the path of a warrior and it can apply to any challenge you have in life.

I'm here to share my path with you. Don't take it as gospel, it's just my way, it may not be yours.

Here's a prose poem Spirit gave to me….

Places You've Never Been

It's okay to cry.

It's okay to miss the one you loved and adored and thought forever would be with.

It's okay to be angry and disappointed and full of rage at me for letting this happen.

You are loved beyond measure and will be held no matter what.

I will hold you until it doesn't hurt anymore—I have no timeline for that.

I will be with you and not look at you as broken, but see your wholeness and strength and fortitude to be here, breathing and continuing to open your heart over and over again.

I want you to know how loved you are, that you are not being punished or condemned or given a sentence.

You are one of the strong ones. You are experiencing this because your capacity is so great—your ability to expand and love is vast.

You are here to inspire and guide others through the darkness because you cannot guide anyone to places you have never been.

Chapter 25 - The Art of Alchemy

One of my greatest strengths and perhaps shortcomings is seeing the absolute potential in people I meet. I see their light and brilliance beyond the conditioning and circumstances of their past. I see their story as the perfect backdrop to emancipation, with no-thing in it out of place. I've begun to see this in myself too.

When I'm smack-dab in the middle of a challenging situation, it's often very difficult to understand how it could be a useful experience for my life. When I reflect on my biggest difficulties I see how they've grown me.

The disappointing injury and illness early on in my dance career spurred me on my journey to know who I was without my identification and sense of self attached to what I *do*. I see how my divorce allowed me to question my misbelief regarding not being lovable and bring healing to that aspect of myself who was living from that place. I now perceive my past autoimmune condition as a gift. With my diagnosis I was motivated to learn how to take care of my physical and emotional bodies through Ayurveda and energy healing. Andrew's suicide propelled me on a tremendous quest for freedom from my suffering, not just from the pain of his death but from all of the preceding ingrained misbeliefs and misperceptions about myself and my reality. My desire to free myself from my mental and emotional afflictions became my priority (and still is). This is the most important aspect of living my life—becoming aware of whatever is a barrier between myself and feeling connected to something greater than myself.

Think back to some of your greatest trials. What were they? List them here:

How did they grow you?

Did you become stronger after you moved through these life situations?

How have they shaped who you are today?

Alchemy feels like the most powerful art form for me to learn in this life. Transforming my most harrowing, darkest moments into energies of tremendous potential and purpose feels empowering and has revolutionized my relationship to loss and change.

Perception is everything. Our interpretation and attitude is the alchemical substance that has the potential to transmute all in our life that we choose. This requires the willingness to see things differently than we have seen them before—to suspend our disbelief, to have a larger vision than the part of us that is identified with the limited, wounded ego.

This may take time, or it may happen in an instant.

The crucial aspect of honing this transformative alchemical process is the heart energy, connecting to feelings of acceptance, appreciation, forgiveness, compassion, love, or peace.

I never used to believe this but have now come to know that from the soul level, every moment of my life has been a perfect expression of the energy I came here to experience and express. I now understand that I can't control everything and when I try to, it's always coming from fear.

Looks can be very deceiving. What may appear to be a great calamity may end up being an act of abstruse benevolence.

One of my favorite ancient parables, shared below, helps me to remember that what I think I see in a moment is not the whole picture. We can never see the grandest vision for our life from where we stand, but having faith in knowing we are exactly where we are meant to be can help to smooth out the resistance and indignation that may feel more compelling than acceptance. It took me a long time for my perspective to shift, especially regarding Andrew's death.

Once there was a poor farmer who had only one son and a beloved stallion, which helped them work the land and earn a meager living. Despite the farmer's lack of wealth he was rich in awareness and understanding of the bigger picture of life. He knew that appearances of good and bad were not always so…

One day his stallion ran away and couldn't be found. The neighbors came by and said, "That's so unfortunate for you that you've lost your horse."

To which the farmer replied, "Maybe yes, maybe no. We'll see."

The following week the stallion returned, followed by a few wild mares. When the neighbors came by and saw what had happened they exclaimed, "What good luck you've got!"

The farmer responded, "Maybe yes, maybe no. We'll see."

Later in the week the farmer's son was trying to tame the wild horses and fell and broke his leg, leaving him unable to work on the farm.

The neighbors, seeing this loss exclaimed, "Oh no, your son can't help out on the farm now, what terrible luck."

The farmer kept calm and said, "Maybe yes, maybe no. We'll see."

Soon after his son's accident, a neighboring army threatened the farmer's village. The young men from the village were all drafted to go and fight against the invaders. Many of these young men died in the battle. The farmer's son hadn't been drafted, as he was unable to fight due to his broken leg.

When the neighbors came by they all agreed, "You're so lucky, your son has been spared because of his broken leg!"

All the farmer said was, "Maybe yes, maybe no. We'll see."

We never really know. Faith is the willingness to trust that there is a greater force in the universe that is magnanimous and has our highest good in mind. This Divine force will hold us through every horrendous experience and be with us to celebrate our greatest achievements. This loving presence is from where we came and where we will return. This essence is within each of us—in our breath, bones, cells, and consciousness.

Can you feel the miracle of this presence moving through you right now?

Notice how this lands with you. Wherever you find yourself on your healing journey is okay. You're not expected or required to leapfrog over any part of your process. Take what feels useful right now and leave what doesn't.

Deep breath in…deep breath out.

Chapter 26 - Awakening through Grief and Loss

Use whatever life brings you to awaken.

I believe that on the etheric plane, long before each of us came into the body we're in, our soul made agreements regarding the path of our life; certain experiences we wanted or needed to have in order to evolve, expand, and remember our wholeness.

These *soul contracts* span the gamut from dark to light. Our powerful soul knew that only experiencing pleasant and cordial people and situations would be bland and would not grow us throughout our lifetime.

Loss, destruction, grief, betrayal: they can be our greatest teachers. We will undoubtedly know who we are when we are forced to walk through the fire. This is the process of refinement. Let life move through you.

I used to be surprised in my Clinical Ayurvedic Practice at how complacent people were. They had indigestion, insomnia, anxiety, depression, or a laundry list of other issues. They wanted to heal but didn't really want to do what it takes to make the changes necessary to transform their health and wellbeing.

Their pain wasn't large enough!

Their need to transform wasn't yet pronounced enough. This is what humans so often do…we wait until we don't have a choice. We wait for the diagnosis, the divorce, the breakdown, the accident—and we don't even know we're waiting.

What are you waiting for?

What will it take for you to wake up?

What will it take for you to live your best life now?

Practice waking up. Be present for your life, for your life is right now. We don't know how long we have here, when we will take our last breath, if we will see our children or speak to our mother again.

Everything is our teacher.

This day matters and you matter. Your life force is intrinsic to the fabric of this reality—if you were not here, the entire world would be different. It will be different when you are gone.

It's so easy to move through life in a hypnotic state. Many people do: depression, anxiety, pill popping, addictions, unhappy marriages, and careers of drudgery. And we've been conditioned to believe *this is it*.

It is only it *if* you agree to it. I invite you to begin to dream and vision beyond what your current life experience or situation may be. Start by thinking of one area of your life that you might like to transform. Don't be limited by figuring out how the change is going to happen; for now, just allow your creativity and imagination to expand.

What would you transform in your life if anything were possible?

What would you stop doing if you could?

How would you like to show up in your life differently?

How would you express yourself, creatively or otherwise?

I've been an adventurer throughout my entire life; that is my nature. Yet in my marriage I became a slave to running a yoga studio and trying to make enough money to pay rent and buy food. Life became a grind. I felt bound to my responsibilities and to my then-husband who had sunken into a depression and wasn't willing to work.

I didn't realize I had options. I thought I had to ride out the unresolved issues of my ex and support him no matter what. I was loyal and assumed that that was what marriage was—sticking it out.

At what cost?

The cost to me was my health; I was in the midst of a seven-year autoimmune condition that was exacerbated by the mental and emotional stress of a vacant partner. My self-esteem plummeted; I felt old, tired, and uninspired.

I thought my divorce would be the hardest thing I would have to endure.

Through loss, I've realized that my chosen path is one of complete awakening and freedom, knowing the truth of who I am and my relationship to my Self and Source. My soul has chosen experiences that, through suffering, would allow me the opportunity to wake up.

A seven-year illness and divorce were not the end of my loss. These experiences merely paved the way for the most excruciating shock and tragedy of my life: losing my partner.

I was so angry with the Creator. *How the fuck could you do this to me?* At the time of life most of my friends were falling in love, getting married, vacationing, having children, buying houses—I was sick, divorced, and then widowed.

Now I see my greatest awakening was through loss and grief. I wouldn't be the woman I am without having had these experiences; they grew me in phenomenal ways. My tragedies became my wisdom, my compassion, my deep understanding of suffering, and my profound desire to live my greatest life.

It may not feel like you have chosen what's happened to you, but I guarantee you get to choose what you do with your pain and adversity. Whatever you're suffering over isn't as important as what it opens within you, who it makes you become.

Turn your suffering into gratitude.

Turn your catastrophe into wisdom.

Turn your calamity into a deeper union with the Divine.

The time to wake up is now. Allow your heart to fracture, your essence to be liberated, and your Self to embrace the dark and the light, the complexity and expansiveness of who you came here to be.

Use your hurts and grief to catapult you forward into the greatest version of yourself imaginable. You've got the opportunity to reinvent yourself as you choose.

The Sky Was So Black That Night

She walked me through the wet grass

Holding my arm to steady me.

Weeks with no food

No nourishment

Left me hollow.

I don't remember what we spoke.

Probably

Ramblings

And hysteria

Of my one love

Vanishing from existence.

Her heart held my pain.

Her spirit saw the truth.

Her love knew my soul's eternal nature.

The sky was so black that night

It soothed me just a little.

I didn't want to go back inside

To the home that was now a shell,

A place where laughter once bellowed,

Music flowed,

And a future was dreamed.

I wanted my life back.

A violent tearing

Broke me

Open

Apart

Away

From the illusion that anything is mine

Or forever

Or as important and real

As this moment is with you, now.

Chapter 27 - Behold Yourself

Going through my divorce in my early thirties tore me apart. It exposed my wound of my love not being good enough and it felt like my very existence was being destroyed.

My ex husband and I met while living in the ashram in India. We were both assigned the task of picking stones out of bags of rice before it would be cooked.

A couple of days before New Year's Eve, it was time for me to leave the ashram and meet a friend in Delhi to assist her on a documentary that she was filming on Tibetan orphans. The day that I left, my British friend didn't show up at breakfast so I never got to say goodbye to him.

"Is it you? Is it you? Is it you?" He asked out loud to his friend, wondering how he will ever know which woman is "the one."

And there I was.

Walking through the cold Delhi streets alone on New Year's Eve, I was drawn to look in the window of a popular German bakery. My nose pushed up against the glass, I peered in. There at the back of the bakery was my English crush from the ashram! Without thinking, I walked right in and up to the table where he was with his friend.

Moments before, Liam was pleading with the universe to show him *the one*. When he woke up in the mornings, he wondered when and where he would find her as he moved through the world. As he called out loud, the universe responded instantly. On the other side of the country from the ashram where we'd met, there I was. Through the throngs of people, I stood before him in the German bakery.

We married three years later. A magical start, perhaps, but the relationship was never easy—strained from the onset by the rigors that long-distance relationships provide.

A year and a half after my serendipitous encounter with Liam in Delhi, I found myself in bed at my home in Vancouver for fourteen days with a disfigured and swollen face, in excruciating pain, and with the inability to eat or drink. It all began the same day that Liam was in a car accident, across the sea in England.

Friends ferried me back and forth to my local hospital for visits and there I was pumped full of steroids and pain medications (the doctors were never able to diagnose what happened). When I surfaced and was able to walk outside on my weak and wobbly legs, I decided that love was worth moving across the world for.

I arrived in Plymouth, England to live with Liam—I was full of hope and idealism. For weeks, I searched for work. I looked for anything from teaching dance in a college to waiting tables. Eventually the latter was the only place I could find a job, so I took it as we were struggling financially to pay rent and afford groceries.

The stresses of being in a place that wasn't my own, not having my sovereignty, and struggling with my health began to take their toll. Nine months in I knew I had to leave England or I would never heal.

Even though a swami friend of ours came to visit from India and told me that according to astrology, Liam would want to leave our marriage, I didn't want to hear it. Liam and I had met so serendipitously, shared the same guru, a love of travel, and the outdoors; it was meant to be, right? This was our forever...or so I thought.

As our marriage began to crumble, an eager counselor coaxed us into a yearlong counselor-training program, touting that this would give us "all of the tools we need for a successful marriage." The one tool it didn't give Liam was willingness. He was so entrenched in his own self that there was no room for me anymore.

For months, my heart broke more and more with every, "I don't know if I want to be with you," uttered from Liam's mouth. Despite giving him everything, deep down I believed my love wasn't good enough; so I kept giving, more and more and more.

I never knew I had an option to leave. I thought "forever" meant forever. Liam broke the dream of evermore and I held on so tightly, not to the actuality of our relationship, but to the idea of what it could be.

The man that I had committed my life to, in sickness and health, was confused and wasn't sure he could be in a relationship anymore. It's always easier to look back with hindsight and see a life-changing incidence with much more grace, perspective, and humor. Unfortunately hindsight doesn't counter the excruciating pain that exists when you're in the middle of something. Time heals.

At least, time is one of the factors in healing. Like meditation, time gives us space between the event or situation and the present moment. We become less self-identified with what happened. The grip loosens and we can choose how we want to feel about something instead of being trapped in the intense loop of neurosis that gets triggered.

Navigating my divorce was treacherous. I sought various avenues for clarity. During an Akashic Record reading I had at the time, the words "Behold Yourself" were channeled. I didn't even know what this meant, but I wrote these words down on a post-it note and put them on my fridge door.

All of these years have passed and I am only now beginning to sense the resonance of what this feels like in my body and life. When looking back, I realize I was living by other people's values and beliefs and I was out of alignment with myself. Through loss, I learned that I had the opportunity to reinvent myself and become aligned with my own values and beliefs.

Behold yourself.

You are the guru.

You are the light.

You are the one you came here to lead.

Life didn't ease up on me until I knew this. I don't mean intellectually—I'm very conditioned and ingrained with knowledge, but *knowing* isn't *being*. Life wanted me to fully become myself and be sovereign in my love of Self.

In my line of work, I've met many spiritual scholars, yogic academics, and walking Ayurvedic encyclopedias. Knowledge is wonderful, but it's shortsighted to believe that *knowing* has anything to do with *how* we live our life.

How we live life has so much more value than what we have read or been taught. It doesn't matter how many years of meditation we've done, how many yoga teacher-training certificates we have, or what letters of proven academic achievement we have after our name. What matters is how we live our life.

The beautiful thing about life is that it constantly offers us opportunities for upgrades. Lately I've been doing some deep inquiry around my values, beliefs, and actual experience of loving myself. When I got really honest with myself, I found there were fragmented aspects of myself that were secretly hoping that things would change externally to give me the life I thought I wanted. Instead of sitting back and waiting for the man, the house, the clients, or the opportunities to arrive, I began to create the life I was seeking. This all starts on the inside.

Do you live in alignment with your values? Can you recall an experience where you lived out of alignment?

Do you act upon your inner guidance? How are you doing that?

Do you appreciate yourself? What do you love about yourself?

Are you willing to allow yourself to change? How are you doing that?

Do you question your beliefs? Can you think of examples of beliefs that aren't your own?

Do you take 100% responsibility for how you feel? How are you doing that?

Holding onto anyone or anything when the universe is tearing it from us results in suffering. But how do we "let go"? If I had a dollar for every time I've heard a yoga teacher utter those words in a class…

Sometimes I want to yell out in the middle of the class and ask the teacher how exactly we should do that. If we could let go, wouldn't we have done it already?

We can't force letting go. Letting go happens.

Sure, consciousness and breath are two powerful tools to assist in releasing tension in the nervous system. Letting go is something entirely different. Letting go is when a shift in consciousness occurs that has an impact on our energy body, nervous system, hormones, and brain matter. When the neuropathways that used to carry an impulse no longer are compelled to do so, this is letting go.

Yes, there are things you can do to prepare for this to happen: meditation, ThetaHealing, Yoga Nidra, Access Bars, certain other yoga practices, and many other modalities.

Letting go occurs where release of effort and control meet conscious preparation. It often happens when we least expect it or when we've forgotten about what we wanted to change so badly.

Chapter 28 - Surrender

How many times in the last week has your yoga instructor thrown in the catchphrase "surrender into the posture" while you were cinched up and twisted, practically hyperventilating? I'm sure I've said this umpteen times myself, yet these days *surrender* has a different meaning.

Surrender is a bit of a dirty word in our society. You're deemed a failure if you surrender, but in the spiritual game it's a coveted objective that few know how to play properly.

I thought I knew how to surrender, like it was something I could check off my to-do list and be done with it. *Surrender. Yep. Check. Done.* But life has as incessant way about it, like how my hamster used to gnaw away at the inside of his cage in the night, surely his version of an Alcatraz escape. Life will keep at us—life wants us to wake up. And someday, the hole will be big enough that it will reveal the light. It's amazing how little that hole needs to be for light to get in…and a hamster to squeeze out.

Life had been gnawing away at me, but it wasn't until my beloved died that I had no choice but to surrender.

Surrender chooses us.

It chooses us through circumstances that are beyond any human or spiritual power we may possess, even though we may convince ourselves for a moment that we can outwit life's reality. "It's not reality that makes us suffer; it's our thoughts about reality," says Byron Katie, a spiritual teacher.

Surrender and acceptance may be siblings or, at the very least, second cousins.

I never fully surrendered to being sick for seven years with an enigmatic illness, and I never fully surrendered to my ex-husband leaving our marriage. I went kicking and screaming through both of these grade five life events. What I learned about going through rapids during my short stint training to be a whitewater rafting guide is that you must steer the raft in the right direction before you enter and then just hold on and paddle like an Olympian to get through. I did neither of these things in either of these mentioned life events. I couldn't. I wanted to be in control, and I hated what I was going through.

I didn't have the wisdom then. I thought the power was in the fight.

After Andrew died, the stark reality of its unchangeable element settled into my bones. I hated it. I wept and I raged. I was so angry with God for letting this happen. How could such a mistake occur? After all the bargaining and pleading with the Divine, nothing changed. No-thing would bring him back.

Surrender didn't come easily or swiftly.

It is only now that I'm feeling what surrender is.

Daily, I'm faced with the angel, the demon of surrender. She rears her head and nips at my heels. She smiles, amused, while I fear that as I've passed over forty and have no sign of an eligible candidate to be a loving father to the child I long to bring into this world. I will be betrayed again by the Creator.

That's the fear. But life doesn't work like that.

As much as I can pray and hope and set intentions and wish, wish, wish—life will do whatever it takes for me to wake up and surrender to Her Will. Can you relate?

It's taken me years to embrace this. A few years ago I would have said that we have free will and can control outcomes. Today, from where I stand, I see that the ultimate control I have is how I choose to be and move through this wild and crazy life. How I feel, respond, act, and show up for life is where my empowerment awaits.

That's not to shirk responsibility or be complacent; in fact, it's quite the opposite. To fully surrender to Her, I dive deeper into the unknown and into the connections with my fellow humans. Interactions have more meaning because I recognize, I will never have this moment in time again and it is so beautifully crafted for me to enjoy...or not. My choice.

In a strange way, this realization brings me a sense of internal relief.

Despite yearning to have a child of my own, I can't force this. Sure I could throw down the ten thousand dollars to freeze some eggs (as some have suggested) in hopes that I find someone, anyone, to fertilize them in the next five odd years...but I see the wisdom in Divine timing and honor the greatness of Her wisdom.

I encourage you, the best that you can, to relax into your life, even if it doesn't look or feel the way you imagined it would. Stay the course and see, feel, taste your deepest wishes until they manifest or not. And if not, at least you've spent your time dreaming great visions instead of worrying about what will or will not happen.

I come from a long lineage of worriers. Not warriors, worriers, I'm afraid. My mother claims she's allowed to because she's "a mother." Fair enough. I may be as much of a worrier as she is when my child is born; but, I have witnessed and experienced how worry robs us of our life force and happiness.

The first time I went to live in an ashram in India for six months, I put my name down to lead a kirtan (call and response chanting) in the evening. This would involve singing and leading over five hundred people in a Sanskrit mantra. It's that odd layer of my personality that is drawn like a moth to a flame, seeking the things that both thrill and scare me. The thing was that I never knew when my name would get called to lead the kirtan—it was like a lottery, and I was expected to be prepared every night. This went on for weeks. One night after dinner I was sitting on the steps outside the kirtan hall. I felt nervous about the possibility of being asked that night or simply not knowing if and when it was going to happen.

A lovely ancient Irish swami who I chummed with walked by and casually said, "Why worry about something that will happen anyway?"

She had a great point.

I was stewing about something that *would* happen in time, or not. I was already overwhelmed and anxious, anticipating a negative outcome. I have been conditioned to think (like many of us) that worry somehow keeps things at bay and is a useful way to prepare myself against a future event's foreboding approach.

Why aren't we taught to visualize and see the best possible outcome for something? Or at the very least, not to pour precious energy into imagined future events that will unfold in a perfect way? Whether it's to our liking or not is a different story.

Exercise: Playing It Backwards into Reality

Sit down in a comfortable position in a chair or on the floor. Close your eyes and begin to breathe slowly in and out of your nose only. Relax your face, jaw, shoulders, chest, belly, hips, knees—all the way down to your toes.

Bring a situation or event to mind that you have some concern about. Notice how your body feels when you call upon this stressful thought.

What would you prefer that the outcome is?

How would you rather feel or perceive this situation or person?

Now, use the power of your creative imagination to walk yourself through the situation the way you would like it to go. See as clearly as you can and with as much actual detail as possible the interactions, conversations, actions, and feelings of your most desired outcome.

Play it all out in your mind's eye. See it all unfolding smoothly and easily. Notice how this feels in your body when you create a positive outcome.

So be it and so it is.

Return to this "dress-rehearsal" many times until the scene becomes known in your mind and body. This will help to create new neuropathways in your brain and give you the option to think and feel differently about a stressful situation.

Chapter 29 - Victimhood is the Lonely Road

Everyone has an opinion about how you should be. None of it matters. They are seeing you and your life through the filter of their own experiences, personality, ego, and belief system.

When I was sick, going through my divorce, and through the initial stages of grief after losing Andrew, I heard all sorts of theories and ideas about how I should feel or be. These came from family members, friends, books, and healers of all sorts. Some of it was useful and some of it detrimental.

I felt like a victim of life, especially after Andrew passed. This was more than an idea; I could feel the victimhood in my whole being, right down deep into my cells. Maybe if I hadn't, even for a little while, that may have been a sign of unhealthy integration of the experience.

I also had an urge, a reason to rise up—because I *had* to be alive. Even in the moments when I didn't want to be on this earth anymore, I knew that leaving wasn't an option, not after I witnessed the devastation that taking one's own life has on those left behind.

I remember sitting with tears streaming down my face, saying to my doctor, "I'm going to have a great fucking life." And I meant it. I had suffered enough. More than what seemed fair. How come other people get to waltz through this lifetime with the glamorous job, oodles of money, hot husband, and tight abs?

They don't. Even those people suffer.

Often right beneath the sheen and perfection, or buried deep inside, lurk the layers of excruciating pain, denial, and unresolved emotions.

Being a bona fide empath, I have always felt others suffering, but now I can actually see it too. I can see it in the luminosity of their eyes, or the lack thereof, and in the tone of their skin that their life force has drained. I can see it in the way one holds her shoulders tense or speaks with just a hint of strain. It's subtle. As humans, we spend a lot of time and energy trying to cover up our perceived insecurities and wounds. We can barely admit them to ourselves.

In our culture, suffering is taboo. We're supposed to be grateful and thankful because we have so much. Yes, we do…AND…by glossing over the emotions of disappointment, frustration, judgment, anger, or sadness, we lose out on the goldmine of power waiting to be re-cognized, relearned.

As Einstein taught us, energy cannot be created or destroyed; it merely transforms from one state to another. The more we suppress the energy of emotion because we feel we have to keep up appearances of having it all together, the more separate we become from ourselves, others, and the world.

Early on as children, we are conditioned to manage our emotions: "Don't cry"…"I've just given you a cookie, why are you still upset?"…"Sit quietly and watch the video." We drug our kids with sugar, video games, movies; any kind of stimulation to entertain them and keep them "happy." From the get go, we train them to look outside themselves for something to make them feel better and calm them down, and their nervous systems get programmed at a young age to seek this external stimulation to self-soothe.

As adults, this pattern continues within us. We believe we can only be happy if the world looks and feels a certain way. This is the road to Hotel Victim-hood. You can check out any time you like, but you can never leave.

This may be the most challenging practice of your life but it's the only game in town.

Without a degree of self-awareness and eventually self-mastery, you will always be a victim and always need to control your environment, people, and material possessions to feel safe and content.

The first step back home toward empowerment is awareness.

We are such a distractible species. Try counting to ten without having your mind wander off to some other time and place either in the past or the future.

Despite having trained in yoga and meditation for years, when I was passing through the intense height of shock and trauma, there was no way in hell I could sit quietly with eyes closed and even focus on my breath. I was merely surviving—from one excruciating moment to the next. Unfortunately I don't have many vices; I didn't have any addictions to avoid my pain or distract myself. So I had to sit in the excruciating discomfort of feeling the intensity of my emotions rise and fall every moment of the day while walking around in a surreal haze.

Meditation isn't always appropriate or even helpful, depending on what you're going through. Awareness, however, is paramount.

First off, become aware of when you're in a mental or emotional pattern of suffering. This may look or feel like negative thinking, aggravation, sadness, anxiety, anger, criticism, and so on. Honor and acknowledge this without making yourself, the thought, or the emotion wrong. You may simply label what you're experiencing. For example, "I'm experiencing sadness." This gives you some distance and perspective, opposed to becoming your emotion. "I am sad."

Once you're aware of how you move away from feeling whole and into fragmented aspects of yourself, you're ready for the next step (if you choose). Before we move to that next step, I want you to realize first that you are a powerful creator.

Chapter 30 - You are a Powerful Creator

Everything is energy. Everything. When you really get that, your whole reality and universe can change. In. An. Instant.

The challenge is that we forget. Maybe we get a glimpse of our energy body during yoga or through another vehicle that allows us to suspend our disbelief long enough to forget about our rent, the problems with our kids, the dirty bathroom, or our aging in-laws.

Imagine that you are a computer, programmed to act, react, and function in a particular way. This is what parents, society, teachers, media, and religious leaders are doing to each of us, and often not even consciously. They are so invested in their view of reality that they program you with it (because it's true, right?). You never get a shot at your own perception of reality…until you create enough distance between others' beliefs and your own experience.

This is what presence does—it allows you a direct experience without preconceived ideas, beliefs, and impressions.

And here's the catch, we are a collection of perceived experiences, beliefs, memories, and cells. The sum total of who you are is a vibration. It's not right or wrong, good or bad.

It just *is*. You just *are*.

And you are constantly changing; new cells are being created, old skin is sloughing off, hair is growing. Every day your physical body is different, so why do you stay captured in your mental and emotional bodies by antiquated thoughts and beliefs that lead you to more and more suffering?

It's not necessary to drag your past around with you. It gets so laborious and exhausting to do so. Freedom is just a perception away. By tweaking the lens you filter through, you can shift your entire life. Do you see your life through the lens of not having enough, being enough, or deserving enough to have what you want? Do you focus your energy on everything you don't have, as opposed to what you do have?

If so, do you think that line of thinking will be useful in your pursuit of the life you dream to have?

You are responsible for your own perception of your reality and for your energy field. The most integral aspect of managing your bio-field, the energy that you are and that extends beyond your physical body, is through being aware of your thoughts and the sensations and emotions that are created from them.

Your thoughts have power. Your feelings have power. You are a powerful creator.

To manage your energetic vibration, you must first of all notice what takes you out of "presence" or out of simply feeling good. Write down thoughts you often have that make you feel stressed, contracted, shitty, depressed, scared, doubtful, angry. Be specific. Write them out as you hear them in your head.

For example: "Why do I always get overlooked at work for a raise? I try so hard and am never acknowledged." Or, "I'm never going to feel better." Or, "Why don't I ever have anything good happen in my life?"

1.

2.

3.

4.

5.

6.

7.

8.

Now, write down thoughts that when you think them make you feel uplifted, happy, connected, free, safe, loving, joyful.

For example, "I love my kids so much and feel so loved when they come up and hug me." Or, "Each day I'm feeling better and better." Or, "I'm so grateful for having such healthy and delicious food on my table."

1.

2.

3.

4.

5.

6.

7.

8.

Can you feel how these various thoughts create different sensations in your body, even as you're writing them out?

Know you have a choice, even though it won't often feel that way, especially when we have programming that is so automatic and deeply ingrained.

There is no right or wrong way to feel. Experience your emotions without judgment or criticism. Often on our "spiritual journey," we learn to separate more evolved states of being with less evolved states of being. This is a big trap. Source is not judging you. In fact, when you feel so-called negative feelings, it is simply your own internal compass letting you know that Source does not see you the same way you are perceiving yourself.

Your own negative feelings are the signal that you are not seeing the situation or yourself the same way that Source does.

Chapter 31 - Find a Better-Feeling Thought

This next step toward empowerment is a process and a choice; not better or worse than staying in a mental or emotional pattern of suffering, but it just feels better and opens you up to more freedom, creativity, and energy.

This next step is one particular mindset tool that guided me from this lonely road of victimhood and brought me back to an empowered perspective and experience of my life. It is gold. I still use this today and feel that this tool can and will change your life for the better, no matter where your starting point is.

If you're cruising along and feeling pretty stoked about life currently, you too can benefit from this life-altering tool. Don't be misled by the simplicity of what I'm about to share with you.

As I mentioned, this is the number one factor that allowed me to heal and pull myself out of the darkness and depression I suffered after Andrew's death.

The key is to **find a better-feeling thought.**

When you commit to this practice on a moment-to-moment basis, it will change your vibration, it will lift you up from whatever starting point you're at. But you have to *want* to heal and transform your life. There may be times that you don't want to, and that's okay; just don't stay there.

Neuroscience has now proven that we can change the structure and function of our brain. This one simple (but not necessarily easy) technique allowed me to reprogram the neuropathways in my brain. I trained myself out of always slipping into the negative doom-and-gloom pathway and into paving new neuro-roads that were more hopeful, uplifting, and positive.

Over time, I have altered my experience of my inner world despite going through hellish external situations.

"How do I find a better-feeling thought than the previous one I had?" you ask?

This is a practice, like learning a new language or exercising muscles you forgot you had.

No matter what thought you are thinking right now, there's a possibility to think one that you feel even better about.

If you're in the depths of despair, you can pull yourself out one thought at a time. If you're feeling pretty good, there is room for expansion to feel even better.

It's not necessarily the thought per se that will change things, but the sensations and feelings that are associated with each thought. Certain thoughts will automatically send your blood pressure through the roof or make you feel sick to your stomach. Other thoughts open your heart and uplift you. This entire inner rollercoaster ride of thoughts, sensations, and emotions can happen right from your armchair, when nothing external is even threatening you.

The good news is that if you have the power to think thoughts that have a physiological effect, you have the ability to choose how you perceive the thoughts that surface in your mind and thus your resulting health and physical well-being.

Dr. Joe Dispenza says, "Your psychology changes your biology." One of the most impactful forms of healing your body and feeling better is to look at the root cause of so much distress, your thoughts, and what you make these energetic thought forms mean about yourself.

There's a woman by the name of Esther Hicks who channels a consciousness called Abraham who speaks a lot about how finding a better-feeling thought leads us out of denser feeling states into more expanded and uplifted energetic states. Again, it's not that feeling depressed is bad or wrong and joy is right, but I think we can agree that joy does feel better. And don't you want to feel better?

Some states of being are denser and some lighter. For me, I decided that I didn't want to spend my life feeling sorry for myself and proving to myself and everyone how hard my life has been. I could definitely sing that tune and be vindicated in it.

We can all justify our pain, anger, depression, and anxiety. I wanted to stop telling that story and recreate my life. I knew that I was the only one who could do this; it's an inside job. And it's work. It takes willingness, vigilance, and determination.

Are you willing to set aside everything that has happened in your past, even for a moment, to experience life without your filter so you can see yourself and your life from a broader perspective?

Here's how I used this technique even in the height of my trauma and grief. Depending where you are in your healing process this may be more or less difficult. Don't wait until life brings you catastrophe; this is a practice anyone can begin from any state.

After Andrew died, nothing seemed to soothe me. I needed contact with people and it was terrifying to be alone. As day turned to night, even more demons prowled as I was forlorn, sitting in our apartment with nowhere to go. I would put my head down on the pillow, desperate to sleep but filled with horrific images of what had just happened and of my ill-fated future. It was excruciating to exist.

But when I could, I would search for a better-feeling thought that would anchor me to the present moment. I would literally become very present to the bed I was lying in and muster up the willingness to appreciate that I had a bed and a warm duvet and a pillow.

My mind then of course would look to what I didn't have...Andrew wasn't lying beside me in our bed and never would again. I would then move my mind back to what things were okay in that moment, focusing on my comfort and safety, without the persistent menacing thoughts. I would again think about and feel the warmth and safety of my duvet cover, remind myself that I was breathing and this was good.

I would remind myself that, if it weren't for the terrorizing thoughts about Andrew dying, everything in that moment was actually okay. This may sound radical, but it's true. It was the thoughts that were tormenting me—what I made them mean about me and my life created all of my suffering.

This is how you suffer too. This is how we all suffer—by believing more in "reality" and our attachment to the stories, thoughts, and feelings that perpetuate an agonizing experience of life. Training your mind to seek out what is good and true in any moment will deactivate the midbrain, the stress center whose job is to constantly scan and look for threats, real or imagined.

Let's go through a little exercise. Choose one thing that keeps you in a loop of negativity, feeling awful or stuck.

What are the thoughts associated with this topic or incident or person? Be specific and write out the thoughts as you hear them in your head.

What are some other thoughts on the same topic that are equally as true that feel better for you to think?

What are some thoughts completely unrelated to this topic that make you feel good? (Hint: keep this as your go-to list whenver you feel yourself consumed by destructive thoughts and feelings).

On a scale of 1-10 (1 being not at all and 10 being fully committed), how willing are you to see, think and feel about your situation differently?

I found that when it was much too difficult to be in the present moment and look for what was truly safe and comfortable, I would move into positive distraction.

The key is to notice when thinking a better-feeling thought on the same topic that you are provoked by takes you back into the negative loop. If this is the case, definitely go to more general topics that you know you will feel good about: think about how much you love petting your cat, or how exquisite the fresh cut flowers on your table are, or how adorable your grandchildren are when they giggle.

Sometimes I would use positive distraction and explore affirmative memories from my past. I would remember going to keg parties in high school with my friends or little inside jokes that only my close family members would get that made me smile. I would even use my imagination to create fabulous scenarios and scenes in my mind. By doing this, I would immediately notice the corresponding sensations in my body—I would be more open, relaxed, and content.

Nowadays when I find myself overwhelmed with a "reality" that feels distressing and I'm lost to find a better-feeling thought, I'll remind myself that "this too shall pass." Because I know that is true. I understand the impermanence of all things—both the good and the bad will pass. This thought brings me solace.

Below is an interesting scale that visually allows you to see the vast spectrum of emotions, and how the higher-numbered emotions feel lighter and easier whereas the lower-numbered emotions are denser. By working your way up the emotional scale, you can recognize that it may be impossible to jump from feeling depressed to feeling optimistic. That's why you only need to think and feel a thought that is a little bit better than the last one. This isn't about fabricating positive affirmations that you don't energetically feel any connection with. If you're feeling blame, for example, then thoughts of frustration are actually moving you up the emotional scale into a lighter resonance.

Baby steps. Don't beat yourself up for not being the most positive person all of the time. You're human and are meant to experience the entire gamut of emotions. This is what makes life so textured and exciting. Just know that you get to choose how long you stay in thoughts that are destructive or move into thoughts that are constructive.

Every thought you have will either expand you or contract you.

Often when we've had enough of the contractive thoughts and feelings (this may take decades for some), when we're so sick of our own heavy story or way of seeing the world, when we've hit rock bottom, we surrender and let go of who we thought we were to embrace a new way of seeing and being.

The Emotional Guidance Scale
By Abraham Hicks from "Ask and It is Given"

1. Joy/Appreciation/Empowered/Freedom/Love
2. Passion
3. Enthusiasm/Eagerness/Happiness
4. Positive Expectation/Belief
5. Optimism
6. Hopefulness
7. Contentment
8. Boredom
9. Pessimism
10. Frustration/Irritation/Impatience
11. Overwhelm
12. Disappointment
13. Doubt
14. Worry
15. Blame
16. Discouragement
17. Anger
18. Revenge
19. Hatred/Rage
20. Jealousy
21. Insecurity/Guilt/Unworthiness
22. Fear/Grief/Depression/Despair/ Powerlessness

The key to feeling better is to find a better-feeling thought than the one you just had. This will take you up the emotional scale. Don't think you need to jump from anger to passion—just move one step at a time. A one degree shift in a different direction has the power to set you up on a whole new trajectory. This will shift your vibration and strengthen your bio-field, willpower, self-esteem, and ability to feel empowered in your life.

It's important to access bodily sensations. This awareness indicates how thoughts literally are related to the responses in your physical body. Thoughts are powerless without the energetic-emotional connection.

Once you have found a thought that feels better, keep moving in that upward direction to generate momentum for your thought forms. Then find another, and another, and another. When you notice a particular thought has bumped you back down the emotional scale, or if you're having a difficult time moving up the emotional scale and finding a better-feeling thought on a particular topic (your ex-wife, money, your aging parents, the death of a friend), then go to a topic where you know you'll feel safe and there is guaranteed contentment.

If you're in a period of your life where you're adamant that nothing (nothing!) is tolerable, then I suggest you look to a positive distraction: go for a brisk walk, take a nap, call a trusted friend, or watch something funny on YouTube.

Some days will be easier than others. This is a practice and not something that happens without a conscious time investment. Just keep going. When you fall down, pick yourself back up. Keep going. Your life is worth it—you are worth it and deserving of peace.

Let's recap the process (which may not always be linear):

- **Awareness, honor, and acknowledge:** notice when you're in a mental or emotional pattern of suffering. Honor and acknowledge this without making yourself, the thought, or the emotion wrong. Label the thought or emotion.

- **Become present:** look around you and acknowledge ways that you are safe and comfortable right now. For example, "I'm sitting in a chair that is supporting me…I'm breathing…I've got a warm cup of tea that I'm sipping."

- **Positive distraction:** think of things that you know you will feel good about: past fond memories, good aspects of your life, a funny movie.

- **Creation:** replace thought forms with ones that are constructive and expansive. You don't have to jump into positive thoughts—just into something that feels a little better and then a little better again.

You can't just think one better-feeling thought and be done with this. It must become the very thing you live for, to find a thought that is going to make you feel a bit better than the one you just had. It must become a way of being that you're committed to in order to gain traction with this technique. I promise that if you invest in this process, your life will change. Without this process, I wouldn't be here today.

This is how you'll increase your levels of happiness and contentment and begin to see the world through a clear lens.

The lens of love.

As spiritual teacher Matt Kahn teaches, we learn to love the one who suffers, love the one who is angry, and love the one who feels depressed. We don't have to love the suffering or anger or depression, just love "the one who…"

That means you bring love to yourself when you aren't feeling very loving. That's Mastery.

This doesn't often happen all at once. It's a process, a journey. How you perceive yourself and your life will change the electrons in your body. Your thoughts imprint the bio-field, and the physical body becomes the replica of the imprint. This is how dis-ease often begins—small, subtle thoughts or beliefs that, drop-by-drop, day-by-day, begin to affect our energy flow. When there is congestion, stagnation, or blockage in our energy field, a physical symptom will appear.

When grief, agony, or loss lives in your heart, you have the greatest potential for joy—a constant reminder of what is important and meaningful and how each day is a gift. Go deep into your pain, just don't stay there. Give yourself over to your suffering, and deep inside you will find freedom.

Life will bring you people, situations, and experiences that you will not be fond of. You don't have to like everyone or everything. Use this grist to reveal the contrast of what you don't want. Let this propel you into greater clarity regarding what kinds of relationships you want to cultivate, and what types of life experiences and exchanges you want to pour your energy into.

Without the darkness, you will not know the light.

Knowing, not evading, the darkness is your greatest ally. Lean into the edges that are piercing—you will find yourself there. From your authentic center, standing in between darkness and light is where infinite possibilities and potential await.

Chapter 32 - Wholeness

I've decided to stop improving myself.

I choose not to let my *prana* leak out, frivolously seeking external validation and acceptance. Instead I focus on where I haven't allowed myself to love and how I can bring more space, tenderness, and acceptance to who and how I am.

All of the other improvement strategies seem futile. They perpetuate the need for an endless cycle of chasing a version of myself that I may never attain, and even if I do, was I really present throughout my life? Or was I always in an imagined future?

Can you relate?

The wounded ego will convince you of all sorts of reasons as to why letting your guard down, accepting yourself as you are, and appreciating and perhaps even enjoying yourself and your life now is dangerous and will leave you behind.

The fear of missing out, being left behind, and not "progressing" at the same rate your friends, colleagues, peers, or society are progressing gives rise to anxiety, depression, and a malaise of discontent. Comparison is the red-headed stepchild that rears its head to make your life unstable and troubled. Its role is to keep you feeling as if you are lacking and seeking more.

The remedy is self-acceptance and love. Seeing yourself clearly, in the same way that the Divine sees you is your pathway home.

You are the very energy from which you came (and will return to). Until you know this in your cells and bones and breath, you will exhaust yourself trying to be someone Better. *Better* doesn't have the quirks and charisma you do. *Better* doesn't have the messy life experiences and character you do. *Better*, in fact, is the epitome of boring, stale, and lifeless.

Focus instead on recognizing your wholeness. Wholeness is the new Better. Calling back each of the forgotten pieces, the rejected parts, the fragments, and the disowned aspects of your being is the return to Wholeness, where nothing needs to be exiled or denied. This is freedom.

This practice needs your willingness, dedication, and presence to have an effect. I've made this practice my life's mission—to see through the eyes of Source. To see myself, my neighbors, co-workers, family, and boss as the Creator does. Sound simple?

It may be simple when they're acting the way we want them to and showing up in a way we approve of, but what about when your child gets thrown in jail, your husband cheats, your co-worker betrays you? To what degree are you willing to focus on your wholeness instead of leaking your energy out in all the various directions of drama?

I'm not saying ignore or become complacent, quite the contrary. Do what needs to be done, say what needs to be said AND, as quickly as you can, call back all of the places you are being depleted because you haven't accepted certain aspects of yourself. When you live from a fragmented state and various parts of you are incongruous, it's exhausting. This often happens when we veto the shadow parts and feel we must only display the light.

It's like having a gaggle of children and only feeding and giving loving attention to the ones you like. That type of treatment gives more momentum to the "bad children" to act up and crave your attention. The same is true with the elements of yourself you've decided or been told along the way aren't acceptable.

What a fiasco that is, and a waste of your precious life force.

But where do those particular expressions of yourself go if they've been rejected? Do they go away? Nope, they get buried deep down inside, and then they get revealed in all sorts of unconscious behaviors: addictions, lying to yourself or others, perfectionism, self-deprecation, anger, depression, or anxiety.

Turn to face your shadow. Know that day cannot exist without the night, nor can light exist without the dark.

Call back all of your rejected inner children and see them clearly, with love. Notice their power, fortitude, and astuteness. What do they want to tell you? What wisdom do they have for you?

Vomiting up your proverbial bad children onto your family, partner, or colleagues won't make you super popular; nor will it have much of a positive impact.

What you do with your shadow is a different story. That's where you will abide in and amplify either constructive energy or destructive energy. Utilize your shadow aspects to restore your power. This will propel you upwards and return energy back into your nervous system and your energy body. Consciously allow energy to move through you, especially the energetic or emotional responses you usually reject or stuff down. Observe when you move into destructive energy, when thoughts and emotions get stuck there. This is an indication of a deep pattern or groove that pulls your attention and emotions like a gutter ball.

Practice allowing small irritations (the polite form of anger) to move through and out of your body. Notice what kinds of sensations you're experiencing that you label as irritation, frustration, anger, sadness, anxiety, and so on. Where in your body do you experience this emotion? And what does it feel like? Is it hot or cold? Heavy or light? Static or mobile? Is there a texture, color, or voice associated with it? Is there something this sensation or part of yourself would like to tell you?

Just ask and listen. This will become easier as you practice this technique.

Exercise: Working with the Shadow

Write with your non-dominant hand and allow yourself permission to connect with your shadow side—an aspect of yourself that hasn't been given room to express itself (fear, anger, grief, jealousy). Do not censor yourself. There is no right or wrong way to do this.

If you're feeling stuck on how to get started, you may like to begin by writing, "There is an aspect of myself that I hate and here's what it is, why I hate it, and how it shows up in my life …."

Notice any physical sensations as you grant this fragmented part(s) of yourself some space and room to have a voice.

Once you're finished, take a few moments to thank this fragmented aspect for sharing with you. Tell it that you hear it and will honor the pain that he/she has been in and do whatever you can to make him/her feel safe. Then ask yourself, "what does this part of me need right now?"

Spring Daisies

Slipping into unremembered lands

Writhing in the pools of psyche

Knowing and not knowing.

Innocence is fleeting.

I forgot who I am

And how She moves through me.

Become hollow

Like a flute,

Her sweet song pouring through

This empty vessel.

My innards scooped away

Replaced by

Illusive and immutable

Spring Daisies.

"Life will not be taken from you,"

She breathed,

Silently, hastily,

Matching the illusion of my trepidation.

Arise.

Arise.

Arise.

Remember who you are

And how I move through you.

Remember who you are.

I am you.

Chapter 33 - The Body Is Your Barometer

Your body is the adult onesie you've been given to prance around in for this lifetime. Whether you like it or not, it's the perfect body for you to fulfill your *dharma* and move through this time-space paradigm.

You may not like your body or particular things about it. Why is that? What do you wish were different?

Every time you condemn your body for not being skinny enough, having too many bulges, too small breasts, too weak, too inflexible, too short or too tall, too hairy, too big or crooked a nose, too small or large a butt, too something, what you're doing in this judgment is giving the middle finger to the Divine, saying, "Screw you, I don't want to be the way you made me. This isn't good enough. I'm not good enough."

Every time you judge your body (or your mind for that matter), you make it weaker and you decrease your immune function. Your cells become deformed over years of self-deprecation and your body begins to break down. Why wouldn't it? Why would it continue to be healthy, strong, and vibrant when you're beating it up and telling it how awful and useless it is day in and day out?

Your verbal beatings may not even be conscious. The wounded ego is very sneaky and you may not be aware of how mean you are being to yourself. Pay more and more attention to the subtle thoughts, feelings, sensations, and stories that you're telling yourself regarding your body.

Your body is a barometer. It is always communicating with you, from the most subtle sensations to full-on symptoms and disease.

In Ayurvedic medicine, it is said that meditation is the first medicine. This is because we must go to the seed, the root cause of dis-ease. Disharmony originates on a subtle level and is the expression of seeing yourself separate from the Divine. When you disconnect and allow your external "reality" to lead you to believe that suffering is more important than loving yourself and what is, you will be caught in hell.

We have been conditioned to believe that happiness is related to how our life looks and getting what we want. This perspective is very disempowering and leads to great suffering, because we will never be able to have everything we want when we want it.

I spent many years feeling betrayed by my body. As you know, I studied contemporary dance at university and was very committed to pursuing this for my career. I was injured early on and had physical setbacks that propelled me on my path to studying yoga and going to India.

This is how the body-betrayal began and led me to believe that God didn't want me to fulfill my dreams of dancing. A few years later I was back in India and got very ill. I was living in an ashram at the time where "selfless service" was recognized as the highest form of releasing us from the ego attachment.

Unfortunately, at the time I didn't understand or have the support to take care of my body and I was urged back to work in the ashram despite being very ill. If you were sick in this ashram you got kicked out; it was as simple as that. So I pushed through. I denied the symptoms from my body so that I would please others and not be perceived as weak or selfish.

It has taken me years to understand that selfishness is not a dirty word, and that self-care is one of the most selfless things we can do. Otherwise, we get sick and become a burden on those around us. That is selfish.

Ayurveda has taught me how to honor my vessel and make my self-care a priority. If my cup does not runneth over, I truly can't be of service to anyone.

From getting sick in India and ignoring my body and then traveling through Asia for eight more months, I was left to navigate through a seven-year illness. No doctors in the medical system could help me; I was left to my own devices. I had gone from being healthy my entire life, dancing five to eight hours a day, to not being able to walk up a flight of stairs without feeling exhausted.

It was like someone had taken the plug of my energy and pulled it out from the Source. Essentially that's exactly what happened—I disconnected from Source on a subconscious level. I became disempowered by believing I wasn't spiritual enough, wasn't good enough, for the Divine. The ashram and spiritual tradition I was connected to at the time amplified these beliefs, and they became deeply ingrained and manifested in my immune system attacking itself.

There was no one encouraging me to take care of myself, heal, rest, and love myself, even if I couldn't contribute to the work in the ashram.

At such a young age I lost my life force, my prana. My conditioned patterns of pleasing, tolerating too much, and putting everyone else's needs before my own amplified and wore me out. I felt like a victim to circumstance, to my marriage, and to the spiritual lineage I aligned with.

In retrospect, there was nothing empowering about my life at that time.

I knew I needed healing but I didn't have the financial means or resources. I moved home, then slept on a friend's floor for months and forced myself back to teaching yoga to try and make ends meet.

What I didn't realize was that my body was communicating to me how out of alignment I had become with who I am. My symptoms were guiding me back to myself, but I couldn't see it at the time.

Disease and illness aren't bestowed upon us to punish us or because we have sinned or need to learn a lesson (although we will learn many along the way). Disease shows up when we've forgotten who we are and why we're here. Symptoms manifest because our body is expressing misalignment.

Illness gifts us with a fresh start—to release old patterning, conditioning, beliefs, and attitudes that are holding us in a state that is not our most optimal state. Sometimes this means we heal our illness physically; other times we heal mentally, emotionally, and spiritually.

If we only obliterate the physical symptoms without looking to the root cause of the mental, emotional, or energetic imprint, then in time we will surely get another opportunity to do this inner work because more symptoms will manifest.

Your soul wants you to live in your most expanded state—your most loving, enlightened, and freest version of your being.

Your soul will do whatever it takes to wake you up.

When you know this and embrace the pain and struggle of what you may be going through, this is grace. Grace isn't avoiding pain; it's knowing that this journey is always for your highest good, no matter how it looks right now.

You can't see the whole story from your current perspective. You have your limited view, your ego's frustration, and your desire of how you want it to be. When your life doesn't align with your desires and demands, you become afraid...so afraid of not getting what you want...and this is why you suffer.

However your life is right now, is how it is. You don't have to like it, but unless you can acknowledge that nothing is out of place, that Source is always with you, and that this too shall pass, you will suffer to a much greater degree.

Experiment with this in your life. Look at your daily, tiny frustrations or annoyances. Can you begin to create some space between the event and yourself? Can you take what is happening to you and see that it is happening *for* you? Perhaps you can't even know or see why some things are happening right now (you're not always supposed to understand).

What has happened in your life that at the time you resisted or even hated, but upon reflection you see how it helped to shape you and grow you in the most profound ways?

Relationships, accidents, illness, death, loss of a job:

What health symptoms are you dealing with in your life right now?

How long have you been aware of them?

What have you done about these symptoms so far?

What is your relationship like to these symptoms?

What might your body be trying to communicate to you through these symptoms?

What beliefs, thoughts, situations, or experiences have contributed to these symptoms manifesting?

Somatic healing is foundational in returning to feeling whole. You can't spend thirty years talking about all of your problems, hurts, and resentments from the past and expect to feel uplifted and pain-free in your body.

Staying present to the body's communication not only honors this incredible vessel you've been provided with in this life, but it also offers you insight into how a thought sets up an entire chain reaction, a cascading of the release of hormones that impact your nervous system, cells, organs, and tissue.

As you go through your day, pay attention to how your body is responding to your thoughts regarding your perceived reality. Do you get a flush of heat when you think about your ex who started dating your best friend? Tightening in your throat as you get up to give a presentation in front of your colleagues at work? A contraction in your solar plexus when you have to do your finances at the end of the month?

Does vitality pulse through your veins when you're out on the slopes on a perfect powder day? Does your heart melt when your child gives you a hug and tells you they love you? Do you get an expansive feeling walking by the ocean as the sun goes down?

The thought-sensation-emotion connection lets you know what thoughts are expansive and which ones are contracting. You get to choose how you allow stress to impact you.

The first step is the awareness of these programmed patterns within you.

Secondly, you need to honor how you're feeling without blaming or shaming yourself in any way. You can say to yourself, "Isn't that interesting how when I think about that breakup I feel hollow in my heart and completely depleted of my energy."

The third phase, once you've practiced the first two repeatedly, is to consciously redirect your thought forms and literally be the conductor of the prana that moves by means of your nervous system.

All dis-ease and symptoms are inflamed by stress. Your body is your barometer of how you are interpreting sensed hardship.

Your body will begin to regulate itself differently when you shift your perception of stress, cease comparing yourself with others, move beyond a "poor me" mentality, and direct your attention to more uplifting and joyful feelings. This happens one conscious thought form at a time. Happiness is a choice that is available to you. This is also a practice, a skill if you will, so be patient with yourself as you move into a refreshed way of being.

In later chapters, I will suggest other practical and tangible forms of working with your body in your healing process.

Visualization: Healing Light Meditation

Sit upright or lie down in Savasana.

Close your eyes and begin to focus on the natural breath coming in and out of the nostrils. Follow the gentle breath in and out of the body for a few moments while consciously relaxing the head, face, and neck...shoulders and chest...belly and hips... thighs and knees...calves and toes.

Bring your focus into the heart space. Imagine, visualize, or feel a tiny orb of light at the center of your heart. See it clearly and notice the warm glow of this healing light energy.

As you inhale, visualize this light expanding in size and intensity to fill your entire chest. As you exhale, relax completely. On your next inhalation, gently allow this golden healing light energy to grow to fill your entire torso, and as you exhale, let your entire body calm. With your next inhalation, see this light expanding to fill your arms all the way down to your fingertips. Exhale and soften your whole body.

Inhale and welcome this light into your legs, down to the tips of your toes…exhale and let go.

The next time the breath moves into your body, see this golden light filling your entire body all the way up through the neck and head…the whole body. Now, welcome this healing energy to surround your body. See your body surrounded by an orb of healing light. The light is radiating out beyond your body and enveloping you in nourishing, safe, and loving energy. Stay with this sensation as long as you like.

When you're ready, maintain the expanded sense of light around your body while returning to the source of healing at your heart center—the aspect of yourself that is unchanging and unconditionally loving.

Take a deep breath in and a deep breath out. Notice how you're feeling. Consciously take in all of the positive effects of this practice. When you're ready, slowly come back into the day by opening your eyes.

Download the audio recording of this meditation here:
www.madhurimethod.com/book-bonus/

Stop Fighting

Stop fighting what is.

Stop resisting what is already here, now.

Stop wishing things were different in your external world.

Stop making yourself wrong.

Stop hating your body, your partner, your career, your illness, or your situation.

Start seeing the beauty all around you in small so-called insignificant things.

Start opening your heart to the splendor of this moment.

You're breathing,

There is life moving through your very body.

You are a miracle.

This day is here for you to rise up,

To know the truth,

That this moment is all you have.

This life matters.

You matter.

You are the magnificence you're waiting for.

Chapter 34 - Doubt the Doubt

I've been told it's there, written in my astrological chart: *chronic doubter*, a label slapped across my psyche that leaked into my nervous system.

Perhaps there's some truth in that; or, maybe I'm human and part of being human is feeling insecure and doubting certain things, especially when there's some previous life experience to back it up.

Doubt can be useful. It helps to slow things down when more space and time is required, but it can also be paralyzing. And for a chronic doubter, it can begin to block the natural flow of goodness that so badly wants to flow through.

Doubt the doubt.

If you're like me and dance with doubt often, use the wild skill you've got to doubt the doubt. If you're so good at doubting then doubt *that* doubt.

If resistance is your go-to, then begin to create new neuropathways and habits that align with greater ease. You cannot connect to your intuition if the habit of doubt is sitting right on your face, suffocating you.

Listening to your intuitive body takes practice; it's like exercising a muscle or learning a new skill. You've been conditioned out of listening to your inner guidance and seeking approval and affirmation from external sources.

Your intuitive body will communicate with you in a way that is unique to you. By slowing things down in your life—your movement, your thoughts, your reactions to people—you will allow room for clarity and a more natural response, as opposed to reacting in tense situations.

Your inner guidance is the connector that works on behalf of your soul. Being the soul's secretary, she is heavily invested in having you receive the wisdom that will propel you forward instead of keeping you spinning in circles.

It's taken me decades to trust and honor my intuitive guidance over my logical mind. The logical mind is useful, but when it's over-utilized we rely on it out of fear; the fear of making a decision that feels right but may look all wrong on paper, to our parents, or to the rest of society.

At this particular time in history and in our culture, the masculine and feminine energies have become out of whack. There is so much emphasis on producing, doing, succeeding, and getting ahead that we've forgotten the power of the feminine. Feminine energy is receptive, nourishing, cooling, and creative. Our power lies in the feminine energy, in stillness, in waiting for Divine timing, and in the intuitive pulses that assist us in aligning with the perfect people, situations, and experiences.

Here's how you can begin to deepen your connection to your intuition and make choices that serve your highest good.

1. Slow Down

If you're going a million miles an hour in your life, trying to control everything and get it all right, then there is no space for the Divine to connect with you. You've disconnected from Her. Slow down how you move through your day, how much you jam into your schedule, how you eat, and how you speak. Make…more…space.

Trust that more space (feminine energy) is the sacred container necessary to feel and be more connected to yourself and your inner wisdom. Space is necessary for communication to exist. Stop trying to run the show. Allow the possibility of co-creation to flow into your life and guide you in the most beautiful ways.

Start with small, insignificant things. Ask to be guided: *Spirit, please guide me today to meet the right people, be in the best places, and have ideal experiences for my highest good.*

2. Listen and Feel

Why is it easier to talk than to listen?

Why does silence and stillness often make us uncomfortable?

Ever been in a conversation that has too many silent pauses for your comfort? Awkward. When you're not present and able to be comfortable with a myriad of sensations in your physical and energy bodies, then you may look for distractions.

To enhance your ability to listen and feel, spend more time alone in silence and stillness, without needing to do or accomplish anything.

This will provide a foundation for receptivity.

3. Ask

You are not alone.

You have an entire energetic support team here with you: angels, guides, ascended masters, and family members who have passed on. Talk to them; communicate with them as you would a friend. Ask for guidance and be willing to hear the answers that come. Or you can go right to the Big Cheese and communicate with Source directly. It doesn't matter what your religious or spiritual beliefs are—and I'm not here to convince you of anything one way or another—but find your way of speaking to the intelligence or power that is greater than your individual self.

Ask for the strength and clarity to hear, feel, and see the signs that are all around you. I always want a psychedelic light show, a mystical extravaganza, to show up and guide me, but this hasn't happened yet. Signs are often subtle and sometimes even silly; they come in mundane ways. You may ask for guidance and then turn the radio on to find a song that directly relates to your question, or you may be in a coffee shop and overhear the word or answer that you needed, or you may see a billboard that guides you.

Stay open to the multitude of ways that Source is communicating with you. You will be surprised. Cultivate this relationship and nurture it as you would any other. Allowing yourself to be guided lessens anxiety and the stress of feeling that you're all alone trying to figure out this life. Open yourself to the support that is here for you; but you must ask.

4. Respond

The classic, debilitating case of listening to your intuition or wise inner knowing and then ignoring it is like a spiritual slap in the face. It's the red flag, waving vigorously and proclaiming, "I don't really trust everything will be okay if I listen to my wise self." Doubt the doubt. Practice listening, and then, please, take the actions that you're guided to take.

The voice of inner wisdom is not pushy, mean, controlling, condescending, judgmental, or harsh. It is clear, often quiet, waiting patiently because She has all the time in the world. But you don't, so don't waste any more of your life making choices based on outdated beliefs, thoughts, or feelings that are not moving you in the direction that feels most inspired, uplifting, and life-giving.

The antidote to doubt is trust.

When you can go beyond believing only what you see and take in through your senses, you expand your capacity to exist in the possibility of magic. Everything that exists in the material plane was once a thought form and, prior to that, an even more subtle vibration.

Envision, imagine, and dream. In your mind's eye, see yourself living the way you want. Feel into what your life would be like in a healthy body, full of vitality, with a clear mind and an open heart. Can you imagine this? No matter what your current state of health and happiness, there is always room for expansion.

Nothing I see is going to sway me from what I trust.

Don't limit yourself to the dimension of the five senses; transform into possibility. There is so much more to this human experience than we know or even allow ourselves to experience.

Through Andrew's death, I had direct experience in communicating with him after he passed on to another realm. Sometimes I would doubt that this was really happening or I would think that I was making up stories in my head. But no, his presence and soul were palpable in both the dream state and waking state for me.

He told me things that helped me heal and understand a little bit more about his suicide. Sometimes this communication would infuriate me and, in the beginning, it would often tear me apart. He was sorry for the pain he caused and had no idea how things would transpire with his family and the way they treated me, but he was seeing life from a different perspective now—from a more expanded and loving place where everything is okay. Perfect, in fact.

I could feel him with my entire being; it was like he was right there. The two of us on opposite sides of a glass wall, reaching out for one another and desperately trying to reconnect, but there was nothing that could be said or done to bring him back to his physical form.

Chapter 35 - 100% Responsibility

Empowerment comes with the understanding that how you show up for your life has everything to do with your perception of it. No matter what horrific tragedies you have been through, you don't need to define yourself by them and let them determine your entire life.

Yes, what has happened in your life is important and is part of your story—just don't let hardship be your absolute.

Life has provoked me in a myriad of ways: Andrew's death, divorce, a seven-year illness, the loss of many dreams, the loss of a spiritual lineage, of a job, of friends, of money. Because of my awesome life challenges, I know moving forward and upward requires taking one hundred percent responsibility for the inner world of my thoughts and feelings and, as a result, what I make it all mean about me.

It took a lot of consistent work to face the demons that surfaced succeeding Andrew's death. They were rascally beliefs that preceded this enormous loss; they echoed back from my divorce and even further back to my childhood.

What arises within you is yours.

Events and situations are divine catalysts to unearth the darkness that has adhered to your psyche, heart-space, and intestinal walls.

It's so easy to blame the external for the misery of the internal. We have been conditioned to see reality this way and attempt to seek refuge in the world of the material senses. This futile pursuit of happiness from outside situations, people, or things enhances the gap between having and not having.

This is pure illusion.

Even if you know intellectually that contentment is an inside job, why does it seem so elusive and far-fetched? Because you've given away your power; believing that when things improve and you have a certain career, relationship, waistline, or income bracket, you can finally feel safe enough to appreciate the fullness and richness of your life.

I invite you to stop for a moment and feel your breath. Feel it coming in and out of your body. Notice the natural movement of the chest rising and falling. You weren't consciously aware of the breath until now, yet life is here with you every instant. Life does not desert you. It's not conditional. What a miracle *that* is.

Taking one hundred percent responsibility in your life is simply choosing how you will respond. Instead of reacting in ways you have before—from outdated habits or beliefs—responding is very different. A response is aligned with who you choose to be.

I'm choosing to be a woman in love with her life, despite it being imperfect, in the face of it not looking at all like I wanted it to or thought it should.

I'm choosing joy, to see the universe as a benevolent place that truly has my highest good at heart.

I'm choosing to wake up every day and be thankful for what I do have, instead of focusing on what I don't.

I'm choosing to live my life with passion and integrity and have love be my guiding force.

I'm choosing to remember that this will all be gone.

What are you choosing?

I am choosing...

I am choosing...

I am choosing...

I am choosing...

I am choosing...

I am choosing...

I am choosing...

I am choosing...

I am choosing...

I am choosing...

Chapter 36 - I Am

I Am. These two words are the most powerful in your vocabulary. What you put after these two words becomes a mantra, a perception, and an expression of how you see yourself.

What do you tell yourself about yourself?

Do you hear the tiny voice, or perhaps the really obnoxious one: "I'm fat," "I'm ugly," "I'm not worthy," "I'm sick," "I'm depressed," "I'm too old," "I'm broke," "I'll never get what I want."

Sometimes this voice is so sneaky it comes as a sensation in the body, a tightness in the solar plexus, a headache, a contraction in the heart, a restriction in the throat.

The practice is to consciously cultivate a more truthful and loving I Am voice, to see yourself the way Source sees you.

Exercise: Creating an "I Am" List

Make an "I Am" list of all the aspects of yourself that you believe are true even if they're not always top of mind for you. This can be short or long. I invite you to come up with as many I Am statements as you can. For example:

I Am kind

I Am generous

I Am beautiful

I Am loving

I Am creative

I Am trustworthy

I Am nurturing

I Am grateful

Notice what happens in your physical body as you come up with your list. Pay attention to any inner voices that rise up to sabotage your expression.

Make your list here:

Write out at least five of these every morning and begin to feel the I Am statements in your body. Get a sense of the energy that feeling these truths about yourself brings. For this exercise, focus only on positive I Am statements that will assist you in generating uplifting energy.

Chapter 37 - Trust

Many humans spend scads of time searching for their "purpose" as though it's a particular label or a certain career, wishing to stumble upon it or figure it out before they can begin their life with any amount of certainty.

Your dhama—alignment with your soul's intended reason for being here—is often broader and more value focused than goal oriented.

You are here to experience the love that you are.

Life experiences will be full of contrast; this is what grows you and allows you to know yourself. If life was always "beer and skittles" as my great aunt used to say, you would not know the satisfaction of overcoming objections, winning against all odds, and mastering an art or skill that seems elusive and out of reach.

Being in the flow of your life doesn't mean it will be effortless. You still need to take action, and you will be challenged, but the quality of your effort will be different. You won't be slogging or grinding it out—unless you're really addicted to this way of being, but it doesn't need to feel like this.

Waking and asking how the Divine wants to move through you is essential; being open to receiving Her is vital.

Living without attachment to the outcome allows room for infinite possibilities, magnificent people, and brilliant experiences to move into your life that are far more spectacular than you could have ever imagined. The universe is complex and miraculous—it has the power to line up exactly what you need, when you need it.

You don't need to try so hard. Breathe.

You don't need to control and manipulate a particular outcome that you think you want. Trust that there is a wisdom far more expansive than your individual self that will carry you through your life, if you allow it to.

It is this very state of credence that relaxes your entire energy field and allows for greater ease and receptivity.

What situations, people, or aspects of yourself do you try to control, either overtly or covertly?

I would recommend spending all that extra time you will now have as you begin to call your own bluff on your manipulation techniques (sometimes they are so subtle you can kid yourself you're not wielding anything) and focus more on the values that are quintessential to your innermost yearnings.

By getting clear on your core values and what you're truly wanting to experience, you're so much more likely to experience it. Funny that.

Instead of focusing on the external goals, refining how you want to feel as you proceed through your daily life can alter the direction you go in. For example I've had various goals throughout my life that once I achieved them it was pretty anticlimactic. I was still the same person. What I thought would change my life and make me feel different, didn't, or did only momentarily. Now I know what I value on a deeper, truer-to-my-soul level. I weigh up all of my decisions with the way I want to experience life, not what I will get out of life.

I value love, freedom, health, adventure, honesty, authenticity, creativity, family, friends, and radical acceptance.

How I want to feel as I locomote through time and space is free, loving, joyful, abundant, and grace-filled. If I don't feel these things then I know something is off, either internally within myself or externally.

What are your core values?

How do you want to feel in your life, day to day?

What needs to shift, change, transform, stop, or start in order for you to feel the way you want to feel?

Chapter 38 - Everything Changes

Everything changes.

Everything.

We know this, yet still there is so much grasping and clinging. Strange, isn't it? The only thing we are sure of in this existence—people, things, situations, experiences, the weather, all of it—is that it's all in constant flux.

The unknown can feel terrifying, but only when we're not anchored in faith and the belief that whatever is happening *is happening* and it couldn't be otherwise. I'm not speaking of complacency here or even liking what's occurring. I'm talking about the fearless attitude that is rooted in love.

To sink into the belly of the natural ebb and flow and rise and fall of all things. To celebrate and enjoy the triumphs and gains but not to be attached as tomorrow you may lose. This is presence.

Wake up. This is your life. It's happening now! Every instant, you are closer to the moment you will eventually leave your body behind, and one day your existence on this planet may be completely forgotten. Don't waste any more time holding onto things you cannot influence or change. Release ownership of past resentments that continue to hurt you by giving your energy and attention to them.

Invest your focus and marvel at the infinite wonders of your soul's journey. I have found that gratitude is one of the most powerful ways to magnify the subtle miracles in my life.

Recently, I had a client who came to me for an Ayurvedic consultation who had built up decades of physical, mental, and emotional toxins.

Along with recommending the proper foods, lifestyle practices, herbs, and breathing practices, I recommended she keep a gratitude journal. She did her best not to roll her eyes and she huffed, telling me she had "done it before and it hadn't worked."

Focusing on gratitude or keeping a gratitude journal isn't about a tedious platitudinous exercise to bore you to death. It's about sitting with the feelings that arise when you focus on what you are sincerely grateful for. It may be one thing—one thing you can authentically feel thankful for. No matter how long or short that list is, focus on the feeling it provokes, and get even more specific about why you're grateful for this particular person, situation, or thing.

Lately, I've been recognizing the myriad of miraculous moments throughout my day, and often I will trip out on being alive. "Wow, I'm breathing. I'm walking around and can talk and move my limbs and interact with other humans and eat foods and drink clean water out of a tap."

When the mundane becomes the sacred, you know you're home.

I encourage you to commit to the practice of gratitude and appreciation; not just once, but daily. Have a little notebook beside your bed and do this first thing when you wake up or before you fall asleep.

Be as specific as you can be, and bridge your thoughts or imaginings about gratitude (yes, you can even make things up if that feels fun and exciting to you) with the sensations this cultivates within your heart.

This practice will increase your *ojas*, your sense of vigor, strength, and immunity. It will train your mind to look for the good in people, places, and things. The world needs more people like you, living in an appreciative way.

Let us go to the next level of gratitude. This is where you go beyond solely focusing on what you love about your life and begin to seek out ways to appreciate the things you've deemed as lousy.

What *can* you appreciate about that annoying co-worker? Or the dog shit on your front lawn? Or being stuck in traffic? (You're stuck in traffic! That means you have a vehicle to drive around in, to protect you from the elements, and even to play music for you. Amazing!)

Notice how the mind wants to focus on the negative, the lack, and what's never coming back. Time to create new neuropathways and light up bright sparkly places in your brain so you're flooded with hormones and chemicals that are splendid and renewing.

When you live your life as an expression of gratitude, you sanctify the very moments that previously you cursed. Grace moves you; you are absolved of trying to fix or change anything; you understand it all as the play of Divine worship. This is Mastery.

God, grant me the serenity to accept the things I cannot change,

Courage to change the things I can,

And wisdom to know the difference.

–Reinhold Niebuhr

Chapter 39 - Healing Anew: Practical Tools for Navigating Loss

The delicate dance of navigating any loss is understanding who you are and what resonates most with your tendencies, proclivities, sensibilities, and heart.

What works for one person may not work for another. Grief, loss, and how you transition through challenging times is so individual. We're all uniquely wired and require different techniques at particular times of our lives. So listen, please, listen keenly to your own inner wisdom. When you're unable to touch upon or access it, then seek guidance and support from people you trust explicitly.

For me, working with all of the layers or *koshas* of my humanness is imperative. In yoga, we would say that you must address all of the layers of the *koshas* or all aspects of your existence: physical, mental, emotional, energetic, psychic, and soul levels.

Food and Nutrition

I address the physical through the lens of Ayurveda, the world's oldest holistic health system on the planet. Ayurveda guides you to the foods, herbs, lifestyle practices, and yoga that are most supportive to your unique body-mind constitution. Ayurveda also considers the climate, the phase of life you're in, the time of day, and the mental and emotional states; absolutely everything that influences your life in order to understand what you need to return to a more balanced and integrated self. After all, Ayurveda translates to the *science of life*.

I co-authored a book with Glynnis Osher called *Your Irresistible Life: 4 Seasons of Self-Care through Ayurveda and Yoga Practices that Work.*

This book will teach you how to live naturally according to Ayurveda and the changing seasons in regards to food, daily routine practices, yoga, meditation, beauty procedures, and ceremony and ritual. I encourage you to learn about your particular Ayurvedic constitution to gain a strong foundation and understanding about what you need to eat and do—or not do—to feel you're living optimally.

Whether you're currently moving through a dark night or not, get your food and nutrition dialed in as it provides the building blocks of stability and optimal expression, not only of your body but also of your mental and emotional states too.

What I love about the Ayurvedic philosophy and system is that it has been around for over five thousand years and is still completely relevant and effective today. Ayurveda teaches you how to understand your unique combination of the five elements that constitute your entire body-mind organism.

There is no one way to eat or to be in Ayurveda, that's why it works—it recognizes how unique you are and guides you to what will be most suitable and efficacious for you.

There are three primary *doshas* or constitutional types comprised of the five elements, and each *dosha* will thrive with different food choices.

If you're moving through great loss, your digestive fire may become weak. You may lose your appetite, notice a thick coating on your tongue in the morning, and feel fatigued and achy in your body and foggy or heavy in your mind.

In Ayurveda, we would suggest not eating if your body has lost its appetite and you're in shock, grief, rage, or heightened emotions of any kind. If you're unable to eat, ensure you stay hydrated and, if you can, drink some broths, have some soup, or sip on some ginger tea. This would be a good start to stoke your digestive fire and begin to clear out the mental or emotional toxins that wreak havoc on your entire system.

I didn't have any sort of appetite for weeks after Andrew died. I just couldn't stomach anything.

I was in shock and my nervous system was only in fight-or-flight mode.

The thought of food made me nauseous. Eventually I was able to introduce food, and I allowed myself to eat anything I felt like—mostly potato chips, bread, cereal, and macaroni and cheese. Comfort food was the perfect antidote at the time.

Give yourself permission to listen to your body and go with it. Know that when your nervous system regulates you will be inclined to choose "healthier" options, but when you're in the trenches the healthier option may actually look kooky. For me it was lots of potato chips; my body's intelligence was craving the oil, salt, and heaviness.

Once my nervous system became a bit more balanced, I began to crave warm, nourishing, grounding, and unctuous foods that were lightly spiced. In Ayurveda, these types of foods are great for decreasing the overwhelm, anxiety, fear, and instability that come during times of loss. This is called a vata-pacifying-food program, meaning it calms and soothes the frayed nerves and emptiness of bereavement.

Listen to your body. Now and always, whether you're going through loss or not. If you find it nearly impossible to do that, learn more about Ayurveda; it will change your life.

Find out more about Ayurveda at:
madhurimethod.com/ayurveda-for-real-life-program/

Sleep

It may sound so basic, but if you've had insomnia you know how crucial getting sleep is and how elusive it can be during times of overwhelm and stress. When the nervous system is dysregulated, it wreaks havoc on the body and mind.

If you are in a time of deep shock or trauma, you may very well benefit from taking sleeping pills if nothing natural is helping you. You must talk this over with your doctor or healthcare practitioner first. Some remedies that I will often recommend to my Ayurvedic clients are as follows:

- Decrease caffeine, alcohol, and sugar, especially in the afternoon or evening.

- Make sure you're getting some exercise in the daytime.

- Eat a larger meal at mid-day and a smaller meal in the evening. This will allow your body to digest your largest meal when your digestive system is more powerful and let your body focus on sleeping instead of digesting in the nighttime.

- Create an environment conducive for restful sleep. Ensure your bedroom is cleared of clutter, electronics, work documents, or anything that will not support relaxation.

- At least an hour prior to going to bed, stop looking at any electronic devices, turn down the lights, play some relaxing music, light a candle, begin to unwind.

- Have a bath with Epsom salts and lavender essential oils.

- Practice alternate nostril breathing to relax your nervous system (see page 186 for instructions).

- Have a cup of chamomile tea.

- Warm milk with nutmeg is soothing to the nervous system and assists with sleep.

- Meditate even for a few minutes before bed. This will help to calm the mind and make the transition into sleep easier (see page 184).

- Write down any lingering thoughts from your day so that you can get any unfinished mental business onto the page instead of rolling it around in your mind while you try to sleep. See page 190 for writing tips and suggestions.

- Use earplugs and an eye cover. This will help to reduce the sensory stimulation and ground your energy.

- Use a few drops of lavender essential oil on your pillow or in a diffuser in your bedroom.

- Massage organic cold-pressed sesame oil on the soles of your feet before bed and then slip on some socks so you don't stain your sheets. This is very relaxing and helps to bring all of the excessive activity in the mind downwards to ground your energy.

- Take magnesium before bed.

- Try taking melatonin (this has the opposite effect for some people, depending what your melatonin levels are in your body already).

- Certain herbs are great to assist with sleep, such as valerian, passionflower, ashwagandha, lavender, and chamomile. But always check with your Ayurvedic practitioner or healthcare provider first, as every herb has a specific effect when interfacing with your unique body.

- Addressing the underlying causes of insomnia is essential to your healing.

Humor

I hadn't heard of Jimmy Fallon before (maybe because I haven't had a TV in over fifteen years). I can't remember how I got turned on to him, but after Andrew's death I began to watch YouTube clips of Jimmy. Laughter. Jimmy's playful manner and ability to giggle at himself touched my heart and provided moments of relief. And then I began watching Ellen too. I had no idea how brilliant and hilarious she was either—I know, I know! I've been living in too many ashrams and am really out of the loop.

I used these funny shows to flood my mind with a wave of comicality, and you know what? I felt lighter! I was taken out of my own trauma for a few moments and reminded of the wholeness of life. Sometimes I would be watching a clip and laughing, only to find myself bawling my eyes out a moment later—the juxtaposition of the high brought me to the absence, to the loss again. But I would play another clip and be uplifted. And another, and another, until the funnies really raised my vibration and perspective. My friend Kate and I would (and often still do) send one another funny Jimmy clips back and forth. Relief.

Laughter is one of the most potent medicines I have ever taken and I will continue to cultivate it.

Find out what kind of humor tickles you. Seek it out and consume it, binge watch, whatever you need to do.

I discovered some brilliant souls who will never know how much they helped me heal: Jimmy Fallon, Ellen DeGeneres, Tina Fey, Amy Poehler, Steve Carell, and Jerry Seinfeld. Thank you, thank you, thank you. Thank you for fulfilling your *dharma* and spreading the light. Stay awesome.

Space Clearing

Everything is energy, even your thoughts and emotions. The spaces you live in, work in, and frequent hold a particular vibration. Especially during times of turmoil, the space in your environment can get heavy, cloudy, and congested. Space clearing is so easy and fun! There are many way to do this.

The most important aspect of space clearing is your intention. You can *smudge* your space using sage, palo santo, sweetgrass, or your favorite natural incense. Simply take a few breaths and get clear on your intention for smudging.

Light your chosen item and walk through the space. With a feather or even just your hand, direct the smoke into the corners of your home, into closets, at doorways, and throughout each room. This is a sacred offering that clears out the past and stagnant energy associated with it.

You may like to use a drum or bell or chimes instead. In the same way, set your intention and then move through the space, using the vibration of the instrument to act as a catalyst for clearing the dull, heavy, or sorrowful energy.

Move Your Body

This is open to interpretation. Walk, shake, run, do yoga, dance, jump on a trampoline, engage in a sport or activity. Keeping the body moving, even a little bit each day, is essential to support the flow of energy coursing through your vehicle. It will also help to lift your spirits and give you a different perspective.

Nature

Go to Her. She will hold your anger, pain, bewilderment, all of it—go to Her and offer up everything you no longer wish to carry. She is that magnificent and powerful. She asks nothing from you and will reconnect you to yourself.

Even if you live in a city, go to a park and walk barefoot on the grass or sit by a tree.

Bask in the miracle of clean water as you bathe.

Honor Her wherever you go, be with Her above-and-below. Remind yourself of Mother Earth beneath your feet and Father Sky above and you will begin to feel more and more connected to your body and yourself again.

Gratitude

This may possibly be one of the most profound energies for inner and outer transformation. Imagine your life if you saw it through the lens of constant appreciation. Are you overlooking things to feel grateful for? You're breathing. You've been educated and can read this book. You've got food and water and a roof over your head. Amazing!

Part of waking up to reality is truly seeing the miracles that are here in this very moment. This is different than sugar coating things or suppressing challenging emotions. I'm pointing to gratitude as an energy, a quality to consciously cultivate in your life. What you focus on will indeed expand, so why not seek out all of the subtle and pronounced things that are life affirming for you? Perhaps there is just one thing, that's okay; start there.

Get a notebook dedicated solely to this practice of appreciation. Go beyond a trite laundry list of things you think you should be grateful for and connect to the feeling state of gratitude. See page 171 for details on how to keep a gratitude journal and work with the energy of appreciation on a daily basis.

Prayer

Nobody ever taught me how to pray—in fact, I'm not sure I even know how to now. The prayers that I recited in church as a child never quite resonated with me. They seemed stale and lifeless, dusty and half-hearted.

As I've gotten older, my prayers have transformed from a wish list to an outpouring of thanksgiving of what I'm grateful for. I now pray for strength and peace opposed to having my life fixed or the lives of those I care so much about. I also send out blessings of love and positive intention to others.

What I have learned is that sincerity is what the Divine listens to. There is no right or wrong way to pray, so there's no need to censor yourself or fit into anyone else's paradigm of prayer. Follow your inner guidance and allow your prayers to be an expression of your heart.

The feeling invoked—not the words spoken—is the prayer.

For the last few years in many of the classes and seminars I have been conducting, I have taught the Ho'oponopono Prayer, a simple Hawaiian prayer of reconciliation that, when repeated, begins to clear out layers of accumulated pain, guilt, grief, and anger.

Ho'oponopono Prayer

I'm sorry

Please forgive me

Thank you

I love you.

Pray with an open heart not a closed mind, and Let your *come-union* be unique to you. As Rumi writes, "There are a hundred ways to kneel and kiss the ground."

Meditation

There's a time and a place for everything—even meditation. I don't think meditation is the cure-all. I believe it can be one of the most powerful tools you'll ever use, but it must be at the right time and in the right way.

I have experimented with numerous forms of meditation for twenty years with varied results and levels of effect. After Andrew's death, it was impossible for me to meditate. The idea of sitting still and focusing on my breath or observing my thoughts was ludicrous and even traumatic. And that was after nearly twenty years of meditation!

So, depending on where you're at mentally, emotionally, and energetically, this may or may not be the best time for you to start or continue your meditation practice. Perhaps you need to adjust your practice according to your current situation. If you're a long-time meditator, be open to changing your practice when required and even letting it go if necessary.

If you would like a starting place to learn to focus, try this effective practice. In this meditation, you begin by concentrating on the natural breath; once a steady rhythm is established, you will incorporate the mantra "*So Ham*" (pronounced *so-hum*). *So Ham* is an ancient Sanskrit mantra that translates as, "*I am that, that I am.*" Such a beautiful mantra that brings us back to oneness where we can see ourselves in one another and know that we are the entire spectrum of Divinity, the so-called good, bad, exquisite, and grisly.

"So Ham" Mantra Meditation

Sit comfortably in any upright position where you can have your spine long but not rigid. Place your palms face down on your knees or thighs.

Begin to feel your physical body. Start by feeling your buttocks supported by the chair or floor beneath you. Consciously relax your lower body, feet, legs, and pelvis. Move your awareness up through your torso and soften any holding in your belly or chest. Relax your shoulders, neck, and all of the tiny muscles in your face.

Now, bring your full attention to the space just beyond your nostrils. Feel the natural breath moving in and out of your nostrils. Follow the breath from outside your body all the way in on your inhalation. Notice how your body moves as you inhale. Then follow the breath all of the way out of your body on the exhalation. Notice how your body moves as you breathe out.

Continue to follow the breath in and out of your nostrils as slowly and calmly as you can. Mentally begin to repeat the manta *sooooooooo* as you inhale and *huuuuuuuummmmmmm* as you exhale.

Continue following the breath and mentally repeating the mantra for as long as you can. When the mind becomes distracted, simply come back to the breath and the mantra and begin again.

Meditation tips:

- Set an alarm on your phone to signal when you are complete. Start with a short period of time, even two minutes, and slowly lengthen the amount of time that you practice this meditation.

- Consistency is where you will begin to feel the benefits of this practice. Even two minutes every day is going to be more beneficial than doing this once in a while.

- Maintain a gentle sense of humor about your meditation practice. The mind will wander here, there, and everywhere. Don't worry about this; simply bring it back to the practice as soon as you notice you're thinking about other things.

To download this guided mantra meditation, go to:
www.madhurimethod.com/book-bonus/

Alternate Nostril Breathing

Your breath is the bridge between your mind and body. Your breathing reflects your mental state and will also reveal where you hold tension in your body. The breath is intrinsically connected to the nervous system. Conscious breathing is a powerful way to transform stress, anxiety, and overwhelm into peace, calm, and clarity. Do this breathing practice at least once a day, if not more, to benefit your body and mind.

The technique of *Nadi Shodhana*, or alternate nostril breathing as it is often called, is a simple yet potent technique that balances the two hemispheres of the brain, nourishes the body with extra oxygen, and releases carbon dioxide and toxins from the system. Stress and anxiety are decreased through the clearing of pranic blockages that lead to disease. This technique will help to balance your prana, your vital energy, for greater focus and tranquility.

This is the perfect practice to do before bed to assist with sleep, or at any time that you feel off center. The impact that *Nadi Shodhana* as on the nervous system is instant and palpable; it powerfully transforms instability to stability and agitation to ease.

1. Sit in a comfortable position with an elongated spine.

2. Establish a slow, calm, and steady breathing pattern in and out of your nostrils.

3. Bring your right hand into *nasagra mudra*. That is, rest the index and middle fingers of your right hand gently at your eyebrow center. The thumb is in front of the right nostril and the ring finger above the left. The thumb and ring fingers control the flow of breath in the nostrils by alternately closing off one nostril at a time.

4. Close off your right nostril with your thumb and inhale through the left nostril. Simultaneously count mentally, "One, two, three, four, five…" until the inhalation ends comfortably.

5. Close the left nostril with your ring finger and exhale out through the right nostril to the same count, "One, two, three, four, five…" until the exhalation ends comfortably (your inhalation and exhalation should have the same count).

6. Now, inhale through the right nostril, again with the same count. At the top of the breath, close the right nostril by pressing the thumb to close it and exhale out through the left nostril. This is one full round. Practice nine more rounds.

For a tutorial on this practice, go to: www.madhurimethod.com/book-bonus/

Presence

One of the greatest challenges you will face at the height of your loss (and simply in day-to-day life with or without loss) is to stay present. Why is it so hard to "be here now"?

The mind is a great time traveler. In a millisecond, it can plunge into the past and ruminate on an event that happened thirty years ago. Similarly, it can leap into the projected future creating all sorts of dramas or dreams.

Part of the process of reprogramming the neuropathways in your brain in order to experience more peace, contentment, and joy is to continue to return to the present moment and acknowledge what is real—literally what is happening NOW. To practice being more present, your inner dialogue may sound something like this: "I feel my feet touching the floor as I sit in this red chair by the window. I'm sipping on my warm tea and I feel my breath moving in my chest. There is soft music playing in the background and I'm aware of the bird in the tree outside the window."

The recognition of what is "real" is useful for calming the nervous system, reminding the mind-body that you are in fact safe (different from what you may be thinking or believing in that moment). This is a skill that can be developed through practice.

Self-Massage

In Ayurveda we have a form of massage (*abhyanga*) where you slather yourself in oil. You can do this for yourself at home. The word for oil in Sanskrit is sneha. This is also the same word for love. When you massage warm oil into your skin, it is a form of self-love. It is a powerful treatment to nourish and ground your energy, calm the nervous system, and help you sleep.

If you are exhausted, overwhelmed, or feeling cold, nervous, or stressed out, choose organic sesame oil for your massage.

If you are overheated, frustrated, angered, burnt out by too much intensity, or in a hot climate, choose coconut oil for your massage.

Here's how you do it:

- Get half a cup of the suggested oil in a glass or plastic bottle.

- Warm the oil by placing the bottle in a pot of hot water.

- Massage the warm oil into your skin. Begin at the extremities and work your way inwards toward your heart.

- Create circular movements on your joints and long strokes over the long bones of the arms and legs.

- Massage your abdomen in a clockwise direction.

- As you apply the oil to your skin, consciously appreciate your body for all it has done for you and for how beautiful it is. It is such a miracle.

- Wait a few minutes or even up to twenty minutes, if you can, to allow the oil to sink into your skin.

- Take a warm bath or shower without soaping the oil off your body (do your "pits and bits" if you need, but try using less soap than usual). The warmth of the water will open your pores, and this will assist in drawing the oil deeper into your body to have a deep-acting and grounding effect.

- Do this as often as you can, just not on your menstrual cycle or if you are ill.

- You can even massage the oil into your scalp, ears, and soles of your feet—the whole shebang. It's slippery though, so watch your step in and out of the bath.

Ceremony, Ritual, and Marking Anniversaries

Ceremony and ritual are not as prevalent in our culture as in some others. This is unfortunate as it's important for impactful events to be witnessed, honored, marked, and even celebrated.

One week, one month, three months, six months, one year…the first Christmas, the first birthday, and the first family gathering can be the hardest after the loss of a person or relationship. The absence can feel amplified and unbearable during some of these markers.

Create a ritual or ceremony that feels meaningful to you and your beliefs and natural expression. I've thrown things in the ocean, burned things, written letters that I never sent (and some that I did), sat in sweat lodges, and chanted Sanskrit mantras. I've had sacred fire ceremonies with close friends and sat on the beach alone talking to the Universe.

There is no right or wrong way to perform your ceremony; do what feels right in your heart, that's all that matters.

Writing

You don't need to be a "writer" to glean the powerful healing benefits of getting your thoughts out on a page. Writing in itself can provide some distance and perspective. It also allows you a safe vehicle to express yourself in any way you choose without self-censoring. This is a great way to move grief, anger, frustration, and depression as it helps to move the energy within you that needs an avenue to be heard.

Remember, no one ever has to see this writing unless you would like to have it witnessed. You are welcome to burn it, share it with a trusted friend, or tear it up into tiny pieces and thank yourself for having the courage to write honestly.

I recommend using pen and paper over an electronic device for writing (but do as you like), because handwriting is more organic; it connects us with our emotions in a way that typing doesn't.

I would suggest trying a few different methods of writing:

1) Stream-of-Consciousness Writing

This is where you set a timer, for say five minutes, and begin to write without lifting your pen from the page. So if your mind feels stuck thinking, I don't know what to write , that's a perfect place to start; literally write down, "*I don't know what to write,*" and go from there. Perhaps the page is filled with that sentence until something else is sparked. The idea is that you write continuously and it doesn't have to be logical or even make sense. This is for you; it's not a school assignment.

2) Non-Dominant Handwriting

For this method, you would write with your non-dominant hand. This allows you to access a different aspect of your brain and psyche that can be filtered out in our day-to-day life. Practice as above with the stream-of-consciousness writing, but using your non-dominant writing hand.

3)Poetry

As you noticed, I have sprinkled some of my prose poems throughout this book. These are all pieces I wrote at various times through my healing journey—from the very raw intense times to the states of acceptance and hope. There is no right or wrong way to write, journal, or express yourself through words. Writing poetry can be extremely beneficial, especially if you find it difficult to talk about your pain and challenges.

Essential Oils

Essential oils are the volatile aromatic compounds distilled from flowers and plants. As potent sources of plant consciousness, they have a powerful influence over the *prana*, the mind, and the nervous system.

They can be diluted in a bath, used alongside a carrier oil to massage into the skin, or put in a diffuser to release the volatile oils and cleanse the space you are in. Be sure to get good quality, organic essential oils that will indeed have medicinal properties.

Some of my favorite essential oils for reducing stress and grounding your energy (in Ayurveda we would call this *pacifying vata*) are as follows:

- Lavender: relaxing, cooling, and calming. Helps with anxiety, insomnia, and increased levels of stress.

- Vetiver: a soothing and grounding oil that nourishes and stabilizes the nervous system.

- Tulsi: known as a *sattvic* (a holy plant) that purifies the body, mind, and spirit. It also supports a strong immune system.

- Jatamansi: (also known as spikenard) is very grounding and earthy. It is said to be one of the best essential oils to support those moving through grief and to release subconscious trauma.

- Frankincense: a highly revered and sacred oil, often used in ceremonies, rituals, and for meditation. Very cleansing, clarifying, and healing.

- Bergamot: this oil is very uplifting for your mental and emotional bodies and helps to brighten your energy.

Flower Remedies

Flower remedies are a form of homeopathic treatment that work on the emotional body to help cope with negative or overwhelming emotions and stress. I have used Bach Flower Remedies as well as homemade flower remedies from a friend. Depending on your situation and emotional state, you will choose the remedy specific to your ailment. Here are a just a few that you may find useful:

- Star of Bethlehem: for past or current trauma.

- Gorse: when you have lost all hope and feel like giving up.

- Sweet Chestnut: when the anguish feels unbearable and the mind-body feels it is at its limits.

- Oak: when you push on without taking care of yourself or taking a break despite the necessity for one.

Bodywork

As I mentioned in previous chapters, the inclusion and integration of the body and mind in your healing is essential for sustainable transformation.

The method is important; however, the choice of practitioner you work with is even more so. Find a healer who is compassionate, clear, and insightful. One who has the capacity to offer you space and who will not enable unhealthy patterns within you.

I work with an extraordinary craniosacral therapist who has been a rock for me. She has done her own inner work and is embodied, integrated, and can clearly reflect myself back to me in order for me to discover my own blind spots as well as celebrate the wholeness of my being.

There are so many forms of bodywork and various healers that I have found transformative: Vitalistic Chiropractic, Emotional Freedom Technique (EFT), Craniosacral Therapy, Access Bars, and Ayurvedic *abhyanga* massage.

Energy Healing

I'm a little bit biased as I am a practicing energy healer with training in Reiki, Bio-Energy Healing, Polarity Therapy, Akashic Record Reading, ThetaHealing, Access Bars, and Ayurvedic Marma Therapy. But I can tell you with certainty that without the energy healing work I received after my divorce and then the loss of my partner, I would not have been able to integrate my life challenges and traumas in such a whole and lasting way.

Without working on our bio-field, our energy field, we can't affect the most subtle and most influential level of our human experience. To this day, energy work is my go-to for keeping myself balanced, happy, and whole.

Most importantly, find a form of energy work that feels right for you and a practitioner whom you trust.

Epilogue

Life will continue, no matter what.

The sun will rise and set, despite your pain.

It won't discriminate and give you only what you think you want. And yet, life is not meant for you to suffer and endure endlessly.

Life will offer you the grandest experiences to break your heart open to love some more— to remember your wholeness.

Through this breaking open, you may fall apart. You may not know who you are or what the point of living is anymore, but I encourage you to take the shards, the remnants, and the fragmented pieces of what was your life and offer it up to the power that created you and will carry you away when the time comes.

Surrender your idea of who and what you are and how your life should be to something more magnificent. I will meet you there, in celebration of your Divinity.

Let's dance, laugh, shed tears, and wake up to the miracle of existence. Don't let another precious moment pass you by without telling those you love that you love them; including yourself.

Be courageous in your heart's expression, offer up kindness and encouragement to those around you.

Be the one you are seeking.

Be the love you are.

Be the one you came here to be.

You are loved.

You are loved. **You ARE love.** You are.

About the Author

Melanie Phillips (BFA, E-RYT, CAS) is a certified Clinical Ayurvedic Specialist with advanced training under the direction of Dr. Vasant Lad, one of the leading pioneers of Ayurvedic Medicine in North America. Having immersed herself in ashram living and study at the Bihar School of Yoga of India, and having taught since 2000, Melanie's embodiment of Ayurveda, yoga, and a multitude of energy modalities has earned her excellence in leadership, teaching, and mentorship for those seeking a way home to their intuitive and brilliant nature.

Having walked a real and vivid healing path through chronic illness and extraordinary loss, Melanie embraces the philosophy that we can all reemerge from darkness and remember that we are all "the light" in our own lives.

Melanie's empathic and sharply intuitive approach helps clients discover the root cause of their dis-eases and empowers them with wisdom and practices to live vital, light-filled, joy-filled lives.

Melanie works out of her practice in Vancouver, British Columbia. She shares her workshops, retreats, and Ayurveda Yoga Teacher Trainings internationally, and also offers remote Ayurvedic Spiritual Coaching and online trainings.

To stay connected or for more information about Melanie's potent, transformational workshops and retreats, online trainings, plus one on one work, visit **madhurimethod.com**

Follow Melanie here:

Facebook: www.facebook.com/madhuri.phillips

Instagram: www.instagram.com/melanie_madhuri_phillips/

For downloads and content associated with this book, visit: www. madhurimethod.com/book-bonus/